CAPTAIN ROBERT A. FRISTER

Flight of the Golden Falcon

Newhouse Creative Group

This book is dedicated to Barbara, my wife, who has been at my side throughout my career. Urging me on through those fifty years of flight. And to the men and women of Eastern Air Lines, whose dedication made our airline so great.

Contents

ONE HELL OF A LIFE

Thick, black, oily smoke surrounded me. My clothes were on fire, my bare arms, my pants, my face, my hair. I held my breath hoping I wouldn't inhale any of it. Still, I could smell that sickening acrid smell of flesh burning. My flesh! It all seemed so surreal. My only thought.

"This is one hell-of-a-way to die!"

1

MY LOVE

It was late autumn, Friday, October 16, 1964. We had taken off from JFK Airport and climbed into a cold, wet, overcast sky that morning. Ahead of us was a three-hour-and-nine-minute ferry flight to Nashville, Tennessee on a charter for the Vanderbilt football team, The Commodores. From Nashville was another two-hour-and-forty-eight-minute flight to Washington, DC where they would play the University of George Washington football team, The Colonials.

The DC-7B, N839, which we were flying, was just one of the many DC-7's Eastern Air Lines called The Golden Falcon, a name the airline used for all of its planes. It was a beautiful aircraft to fly. It had four powerful R-3350's Wright Cyclone engines and fly-by-wire (control cables), flight controls that made you feel as if you were in total command.

We had climbed to our cruising altitude of 20,000 feet and were crossing over the rugged Adirondack Mountains. Some of them reach a height of over 4,000 feet, the view of the mountains blocked by the solid cloud cover we were flying in.

Our crew consisted of the captain, flight engineer, two stewardesses, and myself as the first officer. Up to that point, the flight had been uneventful, routine, just small banter between us in our cockpit and the hum of those four beautiful engines purring in our ears. Suddenly, the calm atmosphere in the cockpit changed when all four engines unexpectedly quit.

Memoirs of flying. More than fifty years worth. Mostly good memories. Some are not so good. All through those years—first as a flight instructor, then as an airline pilot—questions were asked of me. "Did you ever have a close call? Were you ever scared? How much money does an airline pilot make? What were the stewardesses like?"

The question most asked was why I loved flying so much. My answer was, and still is, "When you stand on the ground and look skyward, all you see is the sky. When you fly and look down, you see the world!"

I spent thirty-three years as an airline pilot, twenty of those as a captain. The rest were as a civilian pilot, with three years as a flight instructor. How can I remember all those experiences over many, many years of flight? That's simple.

From the day I first started flying, in the Autumn of 1953, at age sixteen, while still in high school, I was required to keep a flight log that enabled me to keep a record each time I flew. Keeping a log was required of anyone intending to solo an aircraft, or who had thoughts of advancing in the world of aviation.

In that flight log you noted the date, aircraft type, whether it was a single-engine or multi-engine aircraft, the city of departure to the city of landing, point A to point B, including the actual amount of instrument flying, and nighttime flight. You also had to indicate whether it was a local or a cross-country flight. Most importantly, you had to record anything unusual that occurred. It is these logs that help me remember all the amazing experiences of my life flying.

I am often asked, "How do you become an airline pilot?" Depending on what airline pilot you talk to, you may hear diverse answers. I trust that most airline pilots would be willing to educate the general public on how they trekked that long, hard road to be selected to fly for an airline, any airline. Thousands of pilots apply annually for airline jobs. Regardless of their flying background, whether as a military pilot or civilian pilot, or the number of flight hours they may have logged, very few are accepted.

During the years that I was trying to latch onto an airline, most airlines required thousands of hours of flying experience. Add to that excellent health, 20/20 vision, not being older than twenty-seven years of age, and not being shorter than five feet nine inches tall. You had to have knowledge of meteorology, pass numerous written and oral exams, and more before being selected.

As I approached their age limit (27 at that time), I had thousands of flying hours, excellent health, 20/15 vision, and met their height requirements. But still no airline.

Fortunately for me, it was being in the right place at the right time. A day of nasty, foul weather gave me my break.

If I were to write about all of my experiences throughout those five decades of flight, this autobiography would probably have more pages than Leo Tolstoy's novel, *War and Peace*. So, I will condense it—to a very large extent—by only mentioning those rare and unusual events I encountered that were far from an ordinary day of flying.

In this book, I will put you in the cockpit—first as a student pilot, then as a private pilot, commercial pilot, flight instructor, and finally what it was really like being an airline pilot and captain. I will explain some of the techniques and required aspects of being an airline pilot. Hopefully not to bore you with too many details.

This story is not all about me. It is also about friends and acquaintances whom I had the pleasure of knowing and flying with and of some who unfortunately perished doing what they loved. I have included some excerpts from the files of the National Transportation Board (NTSB) and the Civil Aeronautics Board (CAB) referencing these accidents, obtaining them through the Freedom of Information Act. I have also included my personal knowledge. This is by no means to discredit the findings of the Board, but to give the reader a better understanding of what it is like to deal with in-flight emergencies and, with a pilot's main enemy, Mother Nature.

2

OUR JOURNEY BEGINS

My quest to fly began at a very early age. While playing in our backyard when I was no more than five or six years old, I heard the drone of an aircraft engine and looked skyward. Above me, I saw a small yellow airplane circling overhead. As though mesmerized, I couldn't take my eyes off it. From that point on, flying became my dream.

At age sixteen I began taking flying lessons out of a small grass-strip airport in Hackettstown, New Jersey. I continued with a flying club while serving in the United States Navy, based at Naval Air Station (NAS) Brunswick, Maine. Later, I continued to fly out of another small grass airport, Tidewater Aviation, while stationed at NAS Glycol, Brunswick, Georgia.

Upon completing my three-year commitment to the United States Navy, I took advantage of the Korean GI Bill our government offered and continued my pursuit to become an airline pilot. The GI Bill led me to Parks Air College in East Saint Louis, Illinois. While there, I received my commercial and multi-engine pilot ratings. Then it was back to New Jersey with the happy thought that I was now ready to apply for an airline position.

How wrong could I be? By the time I was applying, the airline hiring programs went into a nose-dive and many stopped accepting applications. And I was somewhat naive to all their requirements such as having a certified flight instrument rating and hundreds of hours of flight experience before they would even consider anyone's application, which I did not have.

Eventually, with the urging of my wife, Barbara, along with a boot in the rear, I obtained my flight instructor's rating. Shortly afterward I became a flight instructor for Wings of Morristown, which was based at the Morristown Airport in Morristown, New Jersey. While there for three years, I was building hundreds of flight hours by doing air-charters and teaching men and women to fly, a joy.

As my flight hours grew, I revised my applications to all the airlines that were in operation at that time, and there were many. However, many major airlines began gobbling up the smaller air carriers. When that happened, it usually meant there was less need for additional pilots which sometimes led to pilots being furloughed. A nice word for layoffs.

I submitted to some of the larger foreign airlines, although I had no wish to fly to another country. Their response was no different than those I had applied to nationally: "Good luck elsewhere."

After the experienced pilots were out on the street, many waited to be recalled. Some waited for five or more years before they were picked up again. Others hoped to be hired by another airline. And others simply gave up. Each furlough eliminated opportunities for me to be considered for any airline pilot position. Sadly, many of those furloughed pilots were unable to resume their careers.

Although I applied to many airlines, my heart was set on flying for only one. That was Eastern Air Lines.

That dream came true on January 27, 1964, more than ten years after I started flying. From that moment on, it was a glorious career. I flew for thirty-three years as an airline pilot, twenty-seven of those with Eastern Air Lines until it shut down on January 18, 1991, as did my heart. Twenty-three of those thirty-three years were as a captain.

During my years as an airline pilot, I found that ninety-eight percent of the pilots I flew with were very professional and terrific to work with. Many were combat veterans of World War II, Korea, and Vietnam. A number earned their experience through civilian flying.

But, as in any profession, whether it be doctor, lawyer, or Indian chief, regardless of which airline they flew for, there were, and there will always be, the "two-per-centers" who walk to the beat of a different drum, Unfortunately, we had ours as well.

After the demise of Eastern came Ryan International Airlines (just one of the many all-night cargoes carrying airlines whose pilots were often referred to as "Freight Dogs" as I was). After Ryan came Air Aruba Airlines (under a contract for eight months flying with other Eastern pilots after Eastern shut down). Next up, Baltia Airlines, flying with other Eastern pilots until they too went out of business. Then finally, Kiwi International Air Lines, an airline that was owned and operated by ex-Eastern pilots, like me. Thereto were the flight attendants, ground handlers, mechanics, reservationists, and ticket and gate agents, all ex-Eastern Air Lines employees who also shared in the airline. It was an enjoyable time flying alongside people I had known for over thirty years.

Flying for each airline was different in some ways. Each had its own set of company rules. Managements sometimes differed on their ideas on how to run an airline. The bottom line was to make money and to keep the airline flying. A lot of that bottom line was put on the pilots' shoulders. Especially when the airlines began losing money.

Regardless of the difficulties the airline was going through, you, as a flight crew member, had to live up to your responsibilities. As a captain, there were always written reports to the chief pilot's office when you had an in-flight emergency—such as having to shut down a malfunctioning engine, hydraulic failures, uncontrollable pressurization problems, passenger medical emergencies, and, unfortunately, removing unruly passengers from the flight. You had to note dates, flight numbers, and destinations.

A pilot's flight logbook is a pilot's life diary. His life in the heavens. Each time we lifted off and pointed the nose of the aircraft skyward came that possibility of having to deal with Mother Nature. Take-offs and landings in snow, rain, and fog so thick that your visibility could be less than a quarter of a mile. There are times when your hands are full of an airplane just to keep it straight as you race down an icy runway at more than a hundred forty miles per hour, having to deal with heavy crosswinds that want to push your airplane sideways and off the runway before lifting off. Then you have to land under similar circumstances. Some of them are gut-wrenching, in near zero-zero conditions. Mother Nature can be mean and nasty, turning without warning from the benign Dr. Jekyll to the vicious Mr. Hyde. She vents her anger with violent thunderstorms, teeth-jarring turbulence, and lightning bolts—jagged arrows piercing through the night sky and blinding like thousands of flashbulbs going off at the same time. You hear the pounding sound of heavy rain, hail, or sleet, beating against that thin aluminum tube that protects you as you streak across the sky at five hundred miles per hour. You may encounter heavy icing conditions that coat your aircraft from nose to tail, sometimes starving your engines of precious fuel to the point that engines quit. You're always aware that one moment you hope you never encounter, but sometimes do, will never happen. And those two words that pilots dread, warning that your craft may be slammed into the ground if you do not take immediate action:

"WINDSHEAR!" "MICROBURST!"

Mother Nature is always not to be taken for granted. Thankfully, there are those wonderful moments when she is no longer Mr. Hyde but back as Dr. Jekyll. She is sweet, calm, and gentle, filling us mortals with her beautiful sunrises and sunsets. Her oceans sparkle with white caps against their lustrous background of deep blue. She lets us gaze at those billions of stars that stand out like luminous diamonds against the dark of night. We may gape at the breathtaking glimpse of a shooting star as it blazes across the night sky in front of us. You think you can reach out and touch it even though it may be light-years away—then suddenly, it is gone. You may bask in the glow of the Northern Lights when you explore the northern tier of the United States, on those all-night flights on your way to Chicago, Denver, Seattle, and other cities.

The recollections linger…

3

THE DREAM

Most people will probably tell you that they can't remember many events that happened when they were young, much less when they were five or six years old. But I remember, even at that age, when I first heard the sound of an aircraft engine.

It was while playing in our backyard when we lived at 90 Thompson Avenue in Dover, New Jersey. I looked skyward and saw a small yellow airplane circling overhead and then flying away.

It was shortly after seeing that yellow airplane that our parents took us to the airport in Kenvil, a small town not far from where we lived. The airport had been in operation since the early 1920s and was home to many a pilot who owned Aeronca Champs, Taylorcraft's, Piper J3-Cubs, Waco's, Stearman's (biplanes), and other vintage aircraft that were flown during that time. Today, they are looked upon as the remnants of yesteryear. Today, they are antiques, worth much more in today's market than they were then.

The airport runway was nothing more than a grass strip just long enough to accommodate those small aircraft. My dad parked the family car near a fence that separated the parking lot from the grass field. I remember getting out of the car and standing there watching the airplanes doing take-offs and landings. Suddenly, here came that yellow airplane I saw, or one like it. It landed and taxied up to the fence in front of us. With a blast of its engine, it spun around, its tail pointing in our direction. Grass clippings from the recently mowed lawn flew in our faces from its propeller blast. The pilot cut the engine and the aircraft shuddered as the propeller came to a stop. Even at that age, somehow, I knew that I, a "starry-eyed" kid, wanted to fly.

Unfortunately, years later, the grass strip was eventually turned into a housing development and the age of yesteryear went with it.

Years later, I learned that the yellow airplane was a tandem two-seat Piper J3-Cub, powered by a 65 horse-power Continental Engine. It was the same type of airplane I would fly when I began flight lessons.

For whatever reason, I have always craved excitement. I enjoyed doing what a lot of other guys would not think of trying. I always wanted to see what was over the next hill. I always looked for that next challenge and the dream of flying presented that excitement, danger, and challenge I needed.

I was the second child of five that my parents, John and Margaret (Bertie) Frister, had. Although both my parents were born in America, Dad was of Italian ancestry and Mom was of Dutch descent. Dad was a butcher who managed Louis's Meat Market in Dover. It was where I would work one day—reluctantly, I might add. My mother, on the other hand, was employed at Picatinny Arsenal in Wharton, New Jersey, in the loading department. Think explosives. Black powder.

Dover was a small community in northern New Jersey but rich in history. The famous Morris Canal, active from 1831 to 1848, ran through it. The canal's conduit extended from the banks of the Delaware River, snaked its way through the valleys and farmlands of northern New Jersey, and ended at the banks of the Hudson River. The canal had dozens of locks offsetting the hilly terrain. Barges loaded with iron ore, dry goods, and farm produce were pulled along with the aid of mules until the advent of the railroad took its place.

During its early years, Dover was the center of a vast commercial and industrial region. The town and its surrounding area were also home to Native Americans, the Lenni Lenape, or Delaware Indians, once referred to as the Original Indians. Eventually, they relocated. In actuality, they were forced to relocate about one hundred miles south.

On August 1, 1758, the first Indian reservation in North America was established in Burlington County, New Jersey. This move was ordered by the New Jersey Colonial assembly: "You either go there or else!" Burlington became the permanent home for the Lenni Lenape tribe. However, remnants of the tribe remained in the Dover area. My wife Barbara has some of the Lenape bloodline in her.

Just several miles east of Dover lies the town of Morristown, New Jersey, made famous as the home and headquarters for General George Washington during the Revolutionary War.

Bordering Dover to the west lies the town of Wharton, New Jersey, the home of Picatinny Arsenal (once called Middle Forge), a government ammunition depot that dates back to the Civil War. It was known for being the main arsenal for making cannonballs for the Union Army. Eventually, it would supply our military with weapons for World War I, World War II, Korea, and Vietnam. As a child, I wasn't aware of how dangerous the work my mother was involved with was during those years of war. Before she worked there, a sudden massive explosion killed many people. On July 10, 1926, during a severe thunderstorm, lightning struck the ground, starting a fire. The fire spread to buildings that contained black powder. In three terrible days, a million pounds of explosives detonated, destroying 187 of the 200 buildings. Nineteen civilians and military personnel lost their lives.

Of course, new safety precautions were installed which helped lower the risk of it happening again. But there was always "what if," in the back of the minds of those who were there that day and had to return to their jobs.

Like most of us, those early years are a blur, with few recollections until certain events took place. For me, it was two days after my fifth birthday. Sunday, December 7, 1941.

4

THE WAR YEARS

My parents had been listening to their favorite radio program, while we kids were playing on the floor in the parlor. Suddenly, my father jumped out of his chair and ran to the radio and turned the volume up so loud that it hurt our ears. Of course, as a kid, you didn't know what happened, only that it was something serious by the way they both acted.

Japan attacked our naval base at Pearl Harbor on the island of Oahu in the Hawaiian Islands. I still remember bits and pieces of what the war years were like. You couldn't help but remember. Besides the radio news constantly talking about the war, there were the newspaper accounts my parents would read aloud to one another and then check the obituaries to see if any of the local men who had been called into battle lost their lives. Many did.

The volume on the radio was always turned up when the announcer interrupted the program they were listening to with, "We interrupt this program with a special news bulletin—" I always thought the enemy was just over the hill, causing me many sleepless nights.

The one voice I will never forget listening to was Gabrielle Heater. His voice was always, to my mind, the voice of death. He would begin his news program with the words, "Haa, there's bad news tonight," then inform his listeners about how bad the war was going; where we were being driven back, what was happening in the Pacific, the Atlantic, and Europe, as well as ships sunk, aircraft losses, and the casualties.

As if the radio news wasn't bad enough, there was another reminder that a war was raging. Night-time air-raid drills, commonly known as "Blackouts!" There were plenty of them. The town's siren would begin to wail, and Mom and Dad would close all the blinds, pull the curtains, then turn off all the lights in the house. There we would be, sitting in the dark listening to the radio to whatever program that was on, then wait until the siren wailed again for the all-is-clear signal. All would then return to normal.

During one of those night air-raid drills, my mother accidentally gave me a tablespoon full of red iodine instead of red cough syrup for a sore throat I had. According to her, it was almost my end. Luckily, there was no damage to my throat, and I was not poisoned. Fortunately, I had the presence of mind to spit it all out before swallowing. "And if it wasn't for your guardian angels…" Mom would always insist, reminding my brothers, my sister, and me, that we all had guardian angels watching over us. I believed it then and still do. They, my guardian angels—I say they because I believe I have more than one. And they certainly have been working overtime since the day I was born, protecting me on many occasions when I managed to get myself in harm's way.

When the war started, Picatinny Arsenal went to round-the-clock production of military supplies. Because of that demand, my mother began working swing shifts, as did my father who was hired as an assistant plumber. (After the war he chose to become a butcher and remained one until the day he retired.)

During those terrible years, America's war effort swung into high gear. There were scrap iron, tire, and newspaper drives. We kids tramped through fields of grass and brush searching for pods of milkweed. Inside the pods were strains of soft white seeds that looked like and felt like silk, which we were led to believe could be used to make parachutes. In reality, they were used in life jackets because of their buoyancy.

The war also caused uncertainty. My parents always seemed to be on the job and away from home. A decision was made for my brother Glenn and me to be sent to live with another family.

The Brennan's lived in the town of Rockaway, New Jersey, seven or so miles from where we lived. We stayed there for two of the five years of war, 1942 through 1944. Our brother Ron, several years older than Glenn and me, remained at home since our parents knew he could take care of himself. My other two siblings, Maryann, and my younger brother, Gregory, weren't born until after the war ended.

The Brennans were nice folk and I have fond memories of living with them. I recall waking to the sound of a Rooster crowing, cows mooing in a pasture, and those trips to the outhouse—yes, I said, outhouse—a two-seater. I could never understand why an outhouse would have two seats when everyone wants to be by themselves in the bathroom. In the summertime, the stench could be overwhelming, and it always amazed me why wasps would build their nests in the ceiling of an outhouse. And of course, there was always that fear of having your bottom exposed to an unwanted attack. In the winter, when the pipes in the house froze, and there was no water to flush the toilets, then it was time to put your boots on, bundle up, head out the back door, trudge some two hundred feet through the snow to the outhouse, un-bundle, freeze your bottom, bundle up, and head back to the house for hot cocoa. I'll never forget that "fun" experience.

The Brennans had chickens that clucked in their backyard. It seemed we always had chicken dinner on Sundays. We've all heard the phrase, "Some people run around like a chicken with its head chopped off." Well, Mr. Brennan asked me one day if I would help him catch a chicken for Sunday's dinner. "Sure!" Then the chase was on. Ever try running after a chicken who probably knew the end was near? They were quick, wings flapping, trying to get into the air, as they zigzagged each and every way, with me chasing them. Once caught, it was over to the chopping block. Now, I had never seen the demise of a chicken. Each time it was done, I was never around. That day, I learned how chickens met their end. Grab the chicken by the neck and wring it, or, stretch it over the chopping block. The chicken goes limp as though it knows it is going to be dinner. Down comes the hatchet, and the head is severed from the body. Drop the chicken, and you can watch it run around the yard with its head chopped off, spurting blood all over the place. When it finally drops dead, grab a knife, slit its stomach, remove its guts, pluck its feathers, drop the carcass in a pot of boiling water, remove it, pluck its remaining feathers, prepare it for the oven, bake it, then take it out. Sunday dinner.

All through those two years, our parents would occasionally come and bring us home on the weekends and we would be a family again. Finally, the time came when Glenn and I remained home.

During the week, when our parents left for work, usually early, it was time to get up, get dressed, make the bed, head down to the kitchen, make your breakfast, and head out the door to go to school. After school, the routine was to get back home, do your homework, then you can go out and play and be home by five-thirty. "And, stay out of trouble!" Most of the time when on our own, we would stay out of trouble. That is, most of the time.

Our playtime was with the other neighborhood kids. We played games like Capture the Flag, Kick the Can, and Tag, "You're It." We played Hide and Seek, Cowboys and Indians, and Soldiers. And there were more, many more.

There was no television back then. Our family entertainment came from listening to the radio. There were hundreds of radio programs. There were dramas like *Lux Theater*, *Suspense*, and *Gangbusters*. Some "tear-jerkers" that held Mom's attention were: *The Romance of Helen Trent* and *Old Ma Perkins*. They were just two that I remember. Those programs were sponsored by soap companies, such as Ivory Soap, Super Suds, and Oxydol Soap Powder which is why forevermore these shows are known as "Soap Operas."

Of course, there were wonderful comedies. *The Life of Riley* and *Fibber McGee & Molly* had you laughing all through their programs.

Kids' programs were mostly adventures. I loved listening to *Captain Midnight*, *Superman*, *The Green Hornet*, *Jack Armstrong, the All-American-Boy*, *The Lone Ranger*, *Terry And The Pirates*, and *Hop Harrigan America's Ace of the Airways*. Little did I know at that time that our radio heroes were standing in front of a microphone reading scripts while a prop man made the sounds of horse hoofs galloping, bolts of lightning striking the ground, and soundtracks of aircraft engines. Those shows sparked your imagination. You could visualize all the action taking place and believe it was real.

Then there were the movies we went to during those war years, like every Saturday. Dover had two movie houses, the Baker Theater and The Playhouse Theater. They would offer two movies: the main feature, usually a war movie, and before the second movie started, which was usually a comedy, the war news. It was either *Time Marches On* newsreels or *Movietone News*, with Lowell Thomas reporting. Each showed film footage of the battles raging in Europe and the Pacific. The newsreels continued long after the end of the war in Europe in May of 1945 and the surrender of Japan in August of 1945.

I don't know how many war movies we saw or how many Saturday serials were shown, or how many times Glenn and I would sneak into the theaters when the ticket-taker wasn't looking. We'd pocket the money our parents gave us for the movies and buy candy and soda, always Pepsi-Cola. I still remember the Pepsi jingle: "Pepsi-Cola hits the spot, twelve full ounces, that's a lot. Twice as much for a nickel, too. Pepsi-Cola is the drink for you."

I always thought there were two reasons for my parents allowing us to go to the movies on Saturday. One, the serials were always on Saturdays. Usually, there would be thirteen to fifteen twenty-minute episodes, each ending with the hero facing certain death. You would be sitting on the edge of your seat sure that the hero was going to die, and suddenly it would announce, "Come back next week for the next exciting chapter." And we did, week after week.

The second, and I think the main reason, was that mom had Saturday and Sunday off. Dad always worked six days a week, and sending us to the movies was her chance to relax, go shopping, or visit some of the neighbors. It was her downtime, not only from us but from the strain of working with munitions.

I believe seeing all those movies had a profound influence on us kids, especially those with airplanes. Glenn and I saw the movie *Flying Tigers* starring John Wayne. Afterward, at home, we acted out shooting down German and Japanese airplanes in our imagined Curtis P-40 Warhawk. It was the same plane John Wayne flew in the movie.

One other film that still stands out in my memory starred Errol Flynn. It was another war movie called *Objective Burma*. The movie showed him, and his fellow paratroopers, bailing out of C-47s into the Burma jungle in enemy territory. Of course, the hero came out alive. Somehow, we always found a way to emulate our movie heroes. If they could parachute out of an airplane, there must be a way that we could do it too. Maybe not in an airplane, but something similar. But how?

After scratching our heads for a while, we came up with the answer. Mom's umbrellas. We grabbed umbrellas, climbed up on the garage roof, which stood fifteen feet high, and jumped off. The umbrella worked as a parachute for about two feet before it inverted and was ruined. Mom had a larger umbrella. Thinking we needed more height, we decided to jump off the back porch railing of our house which was two stories high onto cardboard boxes that we piled up in our small backyard to soften our landing. I jumped. Two feet down and another umbrella ruined. We did a lot of extra chores around the house to replace those umbrellas we ruined trying to be our heroes.

Throughout those war years of the 1940s, there weren't too many airplanes flying over our house. Those that did were usually military. Whenever I heard the deep throaty roar of those piston engines—no jets flying around like they do today—I would charge, when my parents weren't around, up the stairs, to the attic, and climb up the rickety wooden ladder that led to the roof. There I would stand in a five-by-five area surrounded by a short wooden railing that protected me from falling off and would watch the planes overhead.

Sometimes they would disappear into clouds and then suddenly reappear. I would watch them skirt around clouds billowing into what looked like huge cauliflower heads, rising to heights of sixty thousand feet or more. It was exciting and adventurous and filled me with dreams of flying. Years later I found out how really exciting this could be. What the meteorologists call cumulus nimbus, storm clouds, we pilots called nympho-cumulus clouds. "F——-g thunderstorms!"

There are special events you remember clearly. I was no more than eight-and-a-half years old on an August day in 1945. Our parents let us roam the neighborhood without the worry of us being kidnapped. "Just be back by dinner."

I had just come out of a deli located on the corner of Blackwell Street and

Prospect Avenue in Dover, a half-mile from where we lived. As I was about to munch on a candy bar and take a sip of Pepsi, the town's fire siren blared. Automobile horns started honking and people on the sidewalks began yelling, "The war's over!"

5

THE WAR ENDS

I noticed a big open-back truck coming up the street. I think it was a Chevrolet. It had a wood flatbed and wooden slats for side racks and was dragging an empty car's gasoline tank behind it. The gas tank showered sparks as it was being dragged along. It stopped right next to me and others walking along the street. Someone yelled to get on board and the next thing I know, I'm on the truck with a lot of others who had been walking. The driver started honking the horn and off we went The metal gas tank resumed its "fireworks" as the truck raced up Blackwell Street toward the town of Wharton. People were waving American flags at us as we went by. Some raced to jump on board but we were going too fast. They fell back and waved gloriously, as in a salute. We drove through some neighboring towns and did not return later that evening when the driver dropped us off from where we had jumped on board.

By the time I returned home it was getting dark, and I thought for sure I was in trouble. I walked into the house and Mom and Dad were celebrating Japan's surrender. I think it was one of the few times my folks never asked me where I'd been or what I was doing. The war was finally over.

Even though the war officially ended, it would take a long time before America returned to being America. There were still days of rationing ahead. To give you an idea of what the effect of the war was like to those Americans who lived through it, and what war rationing was like, my parents summed it all up in just one word: "Sacrifice."

The Office of Price Administration (OPA) began tire rationing four days after December 7, 1941. By January 1942, the Federal Government banned the sale of automobiles and bicycles as the military needed the rubber from their tires. Manufacturers turned their attention to the war effort. Tanks, aircraft, ships, and weapons were the priority.

By May 1942, ration books were being issued and Americans began to feel the first impacts of gasoline and tire rationing. Throughout the United States, the maximum speed limit was set to 35 mph, to conserve rubber tires and gasoline. Each automobile owner was issued stickers that were placed on the bottom left of the windshield. An "A" sticker denoted the lowest priority and these drivers were only allowed 3 to 4 gallons of gasoline per week. "B" stickers were issued to those who worked for the military or had war-related work like my parents. They were allowed 8 gallons of gas per week.

There were other stickers. "C" was for doctors, nurses, medical personnel, and others who came under that classification. "T" was for truckers. The "X" stickers entitled their holder to an unlimited supply of gasoline. These holders were clergy, police, firemen, and civil defense workers. The list of rationed items kept growing. By June 1942, typewriters, radios, phonographs, refrigerators, vacuum cleaners, and sewing machines for civilians were also banned. Almost everything was devoted to winning the war.

Finally, all rationing ended in May of 1946. It had been a difficult time but at last, it was over.

It was the time I attended Sacred Heart Catholic School in Dover. All three of us—my brothers Ron, Glenn, and I—went there for a couple of years, each in a different class, because of our ages. Some of the nuns that taught our classes were not the nicest. I got caught chewing gum in class one time. A nun put a "dunce cap" on my head, stuck the gum on the tip of my nose, and made me sit on a stool in the front of the room facing the rest of the class, where all the kids made fun of me.

Another time, the punishment was a little more severe. I did something, not to the nun's liking, and had to stick out my hand. She broke her yardstick smacking it. She then ordered me to sit under her desk. I had to stay there until class was over. But not before an occasional boot in the rear got me when she sat down. I was never sure if those kicks were by accident or on purpose. When I told my parents about what that nun did, they were livid. It was shortly after that incident that my brothers and I went to the Academy Street School, a public school, just two blocks from where we lived.

The neighbor kids I hung around with lived only up the street. At that time there were no organized sports programs as many kids have today. You chose up teams on your own and played against each other. No parents were involved. Thank God! Sometimes, we got into fistfights. Black eyes and bloody noses seemed to be a weekly occurrence at times, but you patched things up and remained friends.

My memories of childhood would not be complete without talking about the mischief I got into. I was still searching for the action that would someday make me spread my wings.

6

DAREDEVILS

As we grew older, my brothers and I became more independent. On weekends Glenn and I would occasionally camp out overnight at Indian Falls. This was a wooded area, about a mile from our home, where I'm sure the Lenape Indians once lived and hunted. We would trudge up Thompson Avenue, cross Prospect Street, then climb up and down the steep hills that led to it. Our shelter for the night was in what we thought was a bear cave. Although we never saw a bear there. We would squeeze through the narrow opening, open the sleeping bags, and spend the night talking about what we wanted to do in life.

In the morning, we started our campfire. Out would come the coffee pot, bacon, and eggs. Nothing like having breakfast over an open campfire. Then we'd pick up the trash and head for home.

One time, while Glenn, Ed Broadback, and I were cooking breakfast in the cave, we had a surprise we weren't expecting. There we sat, fat, dumb, and happy, frying our bacon and eggs when bullets started going off from inside the fire. One hit the bottom of the frying pan that I held in my hand and sent it flying. The three of us made a mad scramble to get out of the narrow cave entrance as bullets ricocheted off the rock walls along with the pinging sound we heard as they whizzed past our heads.

After we gathered our senses, we thought some older kids had used the cave before us and may have tossed .22 caliber bullets into the ashes left from their campfire. Luckily, none of us were hit by the shells. Of course, we never told our parents what happened. But I suspected Broadback dropped them in the ashes when we weren't looking. His father was a special cop in Dover and had access to that type of ammunition. Although when I asked him if he did, he denied it.

Indian Falls was also home for us to become daredevils. Or "I dare you to," or, if that did not work, "I double-dare you to." For example, "Okay, Bob, I dare you to climb that forty-foot tree to the top. When you're at the top we'll chop it down and you can ride it to the ground." Like fools, we'd reply, "Sure!"

So, those of us who were daredevils would climb to the top of the tree. While we were climbing, the chopping would start, and when you reached the highest point of the tree, you placed yourself on the backside, making sure that part of the tree wasn't going to hit the ground first. The tree would come crashing down, with you holding onto it, and you'd get a hearty back-slap from the guys who chopped it down. Crazy looking back at it now, but it was fun then.

If that wasn't daredevil enough, the next dare was. This time the trees were higher, fifty to sixty feet, branches spread out over twenty feet at the bottom. While a couple of guys attacked the tree with a saw and an ax, the daredevil (idiot) would pick a spot where he thought the tree would crash down and stand there as long as he could before scrambling out of the way.

One day I decided that no matter what, I would be the guy who stayed the longest before the tree hit the ground. I sized up the tree and guessed where it would slam down. As the guys sawed and chopped, the tree began to sway. I picked a spot and defiantly stared up at the tree. Then came that creaking sound when you know the tree is about to fall. It began as if in slow motion, then picked up speed as it fell. There was a loud booming crack when the tree snapped away from where they chopped and sawed. I waited, mesmerized. The guys who were watching began yelling "Get away! Get away!" Too late. I took about three steps. The tree came crashing down around me. Its trunk missed me by about a foot, and slammed into the ground, branches scraping some skin off my arms. Then silence. I walked out of that tangled mess with just a couple of scratches. There was no back-slapping with that one, and it was the last time I played chicken with trees.

It seemed, somehow, that I always managed to get myself into trouble. One day I almost burnt the house down.

My brother Glenn lit a cup of turpentine, a paint thinner, down in our basement, just to see if it would catch fire. It did. Mom was upstairs and didn't know what we were up to. So, to help Glenn put out the fire, I picked up the cup (instead of covering it with something to smother the fire) and tried to carry it outside. The cup became so hot that it was burning my hand, so I dropped it on the cellar floor. The fiery liquid spread, catching some newspapers on fire that were stashed on the floor for a newspaper drive. Glenn yelled for Mom, screaming that the house was on fire. She came running down the steps with a bucket of water and threw it on the fire. Unfortunately, the turpentine, being a liquid, spread throughout the basement, trapping me up against a wall. Luckily it finally flamed out, as did the newspapers, after we kept stomping on them.

It was shortly after the turpentine incident that Glenn and I decided to see why my dad liked Chesterfield cigarettes so much. So, we grabbed a pack of his smokes, went to a wooded area several blocks from where we lived, and lit up. As we were smoking them, Mom suddenly appeared and told us to get home. That night, just before my dad walked through the door, home from work, my mother said to light one up to show our dad how grown-up we were. Glenn was scared to death, but I didn't think anything was wrong. After all, Mom said to light up. Needless to say, when my dad saw me smoking, the cigarette flew one way, and I flew the other. I think I was ten or eleven years old. When we did things wrong, punishment came in the form of a leather razor strap, or Dad's hands. There was no such thing as "time-out" then as a punishment. The next time I was punished wasn't that pleasant either. My dad had me put in jail.

Mom had been saving fifty-cent pieces into a large tin container that had just enough of an open slot to allow the coins to fall through. My taste for ice cream was at a high level—still is—and the local store sold Hershey Ice Cream for only fifty cents a half-pint. I would take a knife, put it through the slot, extract a fifty-cent piece, and go buy a half-pint of ice cream. This went on for about three weeks when my mother realized the tin was getting lighter and not heavier even with all the coins she put into it. My father wanted to know who stole the money and why. My brothers and I denied it. So, it was off to the police station in Dover. Just before we arrived, I gave a full confession.

I was taken into the police station while my brothers remained in the car. My dad had a long talk with Chief Lou Volker who was in charge and whom he knew. The chief, who lived several blocks from where we lived, whispered something to another policeman, who then took me downstairs to the dungeon where all the real bad guys were kept.

The officer opened the door and put me in this small four-by-six room. As he closed the door, he gave me a warning that the water rats were pretty big and sometimes managed to get into the basement of the police station. The police station was right next to the Rockaway River which flowed through Dover, so even if I yelled out, they might not even hear me upstairs. The door clanged shut. The lights went out, and I was alone. I thought my dad was going to leave me there. When they did let me out, which was probably ten minutes or so later, I had learned something: Don't take things that don't belong to you.

By this time, you would think I would have learned not to get into any more trouble. Wrong. I was about to learn something else: Don't hop on moving freight cars pulled by locomotives, no matter how slow they were going.

Dover had the main railway station that served most of the neighboring communities in our area. One of the railroad companies that passed through was called the D, L&W, which stood for Delaware, Lackawanna, and Western Railroad. But it was more known as the Delay, Linger, and Wait Railroad. It had a railroad siding next to Dickerson Street which bordered the railroad tracks and led to the station's depot. It was at this siding where they would park the Pullman cars, coal cars, boxcars, and cabooses. All left unattended.

Glenn and I would go down to the siding and wait for the cars to be backing in or leaving. When no one was looking, we leaped up and grabbed the rungs on the side of the moving cars, one time nearly falling under its wheels. We climbed to the top of the boxcars, ran the length of the roof, then scrambled down the rungs at the other end and hopped off. We might also jump down into the empty coal cars and go for a short ride then leap off, covered with coal dust, before they went back to the mainline. Just another daring episode we learned from going to the movies.

Unfortunately, we got caught by the railroad personnel. A telephone call to my dad incurred more damage to my bottom from the razor strap. All this mischief happened about the time I was twelve years old. But I was beginning to get a little smarter about riding on railway cars. Which we still did. Just don't get caught.

While both of our parents worked, we had our chores to do. It wasn't unusual for us to be washing dishes, washing clothes, dusting, running the vacuum cleaner, ironing, making beds, washing windows, mowing the lawn, cooking, etc.

Usually, we had to make our breakfast because our parents already left for work. My brothers and I had another incident with fire, this time in the kitchen. We were frying bacon and eggs for breakfast. Our stove was gas, the kind where the flames lick the side of the frying pan. Somehow the bacon caught fire. Instead of covering the fire with the frying pan lid to smother the flames (you would think we would have learned that after the basement fiasco), we tried to carry the burning pan out the back door. We would have made it if we did not trip and spill the burning grease on the kitchen floor which was linoleum. Burning linoleum has an acrid smell and turns black when on fire. We hurriedly put out the fire, but it left a gummy mess on the bottom of our shoes when our shoes acted as a fire extinguisher. Our parents weren't too happy about that incident either.

7

BALSA PLANES AND BEYOND

Remember those balsa wood airplanes you could buy for just a dime? You put them together by sliding the wings through a slit in the thin wood fuselage. You would attach the horizontal stabilizer, stick the rudder on, and presto, you had an airplane to fly. Most of the time, you'd see if you could get it to do aerobatics such as loops and steep turns. But the main goal was to see if your airplane could glide farther than those of the other guys. We would also build model airplanes that came in kits and laboriously put them together using plastic glue.

You would think putting balsa wood airplanes together couldn't get you into trouble, right? Wrong. The glue was flammable, so we would spread it over the wings of the balsa wood airplanes, light the glue, and send the airplane soaring, making believe it was an enemy aircraft and was being shot down. When we did that to five of those airplanes, we were considered aces. However, all that came to an end when we sent a couple of the burning planes into a dried-out grass field on a windy day. It took about fifteen minutes before the fire department showed up. By the time the fire reached the woods, we were back home. But there was no more shooting down enemy airplanes.

But there were those real .049 gas and propeller-driven model airplanes guys would fly. Most of them were controlled by the use of hand-held wire flight controls. Remote control aircraft were few and far between at that time. Glenn and I happened to be down at Hamilton Field in Dover where the Dover High School held its football games. Except on that day, there was no football. Instead, several guys were flying their gas model airplanes on a field just outside the football field. The guy who was to fly his model stood in the middle of the field, the control cables laid out to their maximum. Another guy was to start the engine and then get out of the way. If you have never heard a .049 engine at its peak revolutions, think swarms of angry bees chasing you. You would not believe how fast a propeller-driven, low-wing model aircraft can zip around in a circle. It can be quite exciting and very dangerous. These model airplanes can reach speeds of more than sixty miles per hour.

Just before the owner prepared to start the engine, he warned us kids to either get behind a car parked on the field or get under it, just in case the wire broke. We decided to slide under the car. That was when you had plenty of headroom underneath car chassis. He started the engine and ran and stood by the side of the car, not behind it as the other guy did.

We watched as the model airplane zoomed, first high, then low, to where it was just skimming the ground, then soared back to level flight. You could see the strain on the man's arm flying it as the model soared around in its arc. It was at its max speed, its propeller spinning at thousands of revolutions per minute. As it headed in our direction, the control wires snapped. We buried our heads in the dirt. Then we heard that sickening smack as it hit the guy standing next to the car square in the face. It happened so fast he didn't have time to react, only to scream. His face was a bloody mess. The guy flying the model and another guy grabbed him and put him in the car we were under. When the engine started, we scrambled out from underneath to keep from being run over. Then we watched the car, tires spinning and dirt flying, speed off toward Dover General Hospital, two miles away. We heard days later that the man died from his injuries.

I have a great taste for coffee which I began drinking around the age of five. At this time, my mother had an electric percolator. One day she told me that the percolator might have a short in it, so don't use it. Sure! No sooner did she leave the kitchen than I had this bright idea on how to fix it.

27

You would think by this time, much older, I would have some smarts on what not to do. Wrong again. I filled the percolator with water and plugged it in. Then I stuck my hand down inside and grabbed hold of the bottom of the percolator's stem and wiggled it back and forth to see if that was the problem. Pointless to say, I got knocked on my a— from the electric shock. I thanked my guardian angels I wasn't electrocuted. Mom got rid of it when she decided it couldn't be fixed. I never told anyone how stupid I was in trying to fix it.

When World War II ended, times became better. Gone was gasoline rationing. The A and B stickers on my parent's car came off. Food rationing stamps began to disappear. Life was getting back to normal.

As we grew older, my brothers and I traded in our cap-pistols that we used to play Cowboys and Indians, or cops and robbers. We gave up playing soldiers fighting the enemy. However, television was coming into its own. The biggie was the Red Ryder show.

You could buy a Red Ryder BB Gun and shoot at targets with a big black bullseye. Purchasing a BB gun was easy depending on your age. Some of the older guys owned .22 caliber rifles or handguns. They usually went to Indian Falls for target practice. Our gang, The Thompson Hill Gang, was well known in Dover, as were other so-called gangs that were in the neighboring towns of Mine Hill, Kenvil, Wharton, and Roxbury. None of our gangs were anything like the bands you read about that attack one another for territorial control. We were the kind that bonded together and played football, baseball, basketball, and pond hockey against one another.

We never expected any of us would commit a murder.

8

A SAD ENDING

Growing up you learn a little about life and death, and about people you think you know but don't. There is a saying that says, "Guns don't kill people. People kill people." One of the guys I used to hang around with was Billy Nickle. Billy was a sixteen-year-old Sophomore and several years older than me. He wore thick glasses and had a bad case of acne. I thought he was a nice guy and we always got along. However, some of the older guys would pick on him. Even though Billy was shorter than most of the guys his age, he would never back down. Before the fight started, off would come his glasses. I thought by doing that, he gave himself a huge disadvantage. Of course, he was always on the losing end of the fights.

I remember on several occasions when he would take his aunt's car, without her permission, from where she parked it in a garage several blocks from where they lived. Then Billy would pick up a bunch of us kids and we'd go "joyriding." We all had a great time, riding around, not thinking of the consequences. This went on for some time until he got caught. Luckily, I wasn't with him when he did. I was not concerned about what his aunt would do to me, but what my dad would do if he found out that I went "joyriding" with him.

Billy lived with his aunt and uncle on Academy Street, directly across from the school we attended, which I could see from where I lived. It wasn't long after that car incident that he got caught doing something a lot more serious.

One evening Billy and I were hanging around Eisner's Market. Eisner's was a local grocery store located on William Street, between Thompson Avenue and Academy Street. Just before the store closed that Saturday night, we said our goodnights and headed back to our homes. It would be the last time I saw Billy, except for his pictures in the local and New York newspapers.

April 2, 1951.

My bedroom was in the back of the house on the second floor. When I awoke, I always looked out the window to see what the weather was like. As I glanced up the hill where Billy lived, I saw a gathering of police cars, ambulances, and news-media trucks.

I learned later that after he left me that afternoon, Billy went home, retrieved a .22 caliber rifle, and waited.

According to Billy's statement to the police, he shot and killed another aunt who was visiting with his family while she was dozing in a chair.

Billy then went into the bedroom where his uncle lay dying of cancer. He shot and killed him.

Then Billy waited for the aunt whose car he had been taking on our "joyrides" to return home.

Billy shot and killed his aunt as she came through the front door.

Because Billy was sixteen, he was not given the death penalty. Instead, he received a life jail sentence for each murder.

At first, I did not believe my friend could do something like this. Nobody could believe it. It was a sad, sad, conclusion to a young life. It made me realize that people were capable of almost anything. I needed to find myself.

9

BOB THE BUTCHER?

y parents had a new home built. We moved from 90 Thompson Ave to 33 Knickerbocker Avenue which was less than a half-mile away from our former home, still in the town of Dover. That meant my brothers and I was still able to hang around with the guys from the neighborhood.

The move happened about the time I received my working papers. My father, being the manager of Louis's Meat Market in Dover, put me to work there. I say "put" because I had no choice. Back then, you worked where your father said. The job paid about 60 cents an hour. Even before that job, as we were growing up, Dad made sure we guys always had some sort of job. If we did not, he would find one for us. Whether it was cutting grass in the neighborhood, a newspaper route, shoveling sidewalks and driveways when it snowed, or collecting newspapers and taking them down to a local junkyard that paid by the pound for them, we all had to work.

There was a trick we learned to make the weight of newspapers heavier. Not from Dad. We would soak some of the newspapers with water and bury them between the dry ones, making the tied bundle heavier and getting us more money. That worked for a while until we got caught doing it by the guy who bought the papers from us.

That wasn't the only thing that we got caught doing. Every April, Dover would sponsor an opening day of fishing for Trout in the Rockaway River. If you have never seen an opening day, just imagine hundreds of fishing poles up and down the river. Lines tangled, tempers flared, but whoever caught the biggest fish, or the fish that weighed the most, would win a prize. Catching the biggest fish was the most difficult. Having the heaviest fish was easy: just stuff as many BBs as you could down its throat. The more BBs, the heavier the fish. We were caught and disqualified.

Louis's Meat Market was located on Blackwell Street and backed up to the Rockaway River behind it. One of the jobs I had at the store was to put down sawdust on the floor to dry up the blood that came from the butchered and trimmed meat. They kept the bags of sawdust in a crawl space below the main floor and I would have to go down and bring them up. Remember the police station story? One day while I was down there, I saw a pair of eyes staring at me from a dark corner. It was the biggest water rat I had ever seen followed by my hasty retreat. That rat must have measured at least two feet long from its nose to the end of its tail. The next time I had to go down there it was with a meat cleaver in my hand.

My job included cleaning out the cans that held trimmed fat off meat that was thrown away. They smelled pretty ripe by closing time. I also had the job of making hamburger patties and carrying hindquarters of beef that could weigh 170 pounds or more. Dad would sometimes let me bone meat. He warned me to bone the meat with the knife moving away from you, never toward you, so you would not accidentally stab yourself in the stomach. I don't think it was more than a couple of days after that warning that Herb, one of the butchers, stabbed himself in the stomach with a six-inch knife by boning toward himself. There was a lot of blood coming out of that wound. He was raced to the hospital and survived. But he did it again several months later, the same drill, to the hospital, and then back to work. Some guys never learn.

Once I acquired my driver's license, Dad would let me drive the market's delivery trucks. I would take the meat orders to the restaurants that he had as customers. The kitchen of some of those restaurants was eye-opening. Most were spic-and-span. Others? Don't go there to eat.

The truck would also be used to pick up hindquarters of meat that were ordered from meatpacking houses in Hoboken, New Jersey, or on Canal Street in New York City. Canal Street then had all the makings of a truck circus. Refrigerated tractor-trailers, box trucks, and vans, all vying to back into the loading ramps, to load, or off-load, tons of butchered meat. All these trucks had to wait in line for their turn. But for some reason, the managers of these companies went out of their way to help me park the one-ton truck. They got me loaded ahead of the line of trucks that had been waiting and sent me on my way. The other truckers did not seem to mind and were friendly toward me. I don't know whether it was because of my young age, or because it only took a matter of minutes to load the truck.

I learned to respect the hard work of my dad and the other butchers. They had to be careful with the equipment or they could die or be severely injured. Did my dad love his work? Did the others? They did it for their families and I respected that too. But as I worked on all these jobs, I knew I wanted something else for myself.

10

EYES ON THE SKY

Time and tide, as we all know, wait for no one. I was in a hurry to find out who I was.

In high school, I played the trumpet in the band, marched at football games, gave up the trumpet, played track, and football. I got kicked off the football team after chiding the coach for not taking out the left tackle for missing too many tackles. It happened to be the same position I played. It seemed I never learned to keep my mouth shut. I took up trying to play the guitar but gave that up too. During those four long years of high school, I would spend some of my one-hour study periods in the library.

The library had a nice selection of famous novels which I would read when I put aside the homework I should have been doing. Leo Tolstoy's *War and Peace* took me two years of one-hour study halls to read the 1,225-page novel. John Steinbeck's *Of Mice and Men*, Jack London's *White Fang*, and *They Fought for The Sky* by Quentin Reynolds were all read in the same way.

Reynolds's writing of World War I combat in the skies over Europe made me read more about America's Flying Aces. My hero at the time was Captain Eddie Rickenbacker who shot down 26 enemy airplanes during "The War to End All Wars." The "Hat-In-The-Ring" 94th Aero Squadron was Rickenbacker's squadron and the most famous. Captain Eddie would later become the owner of Eastern Air Lines. The Hat-In-The-Ring would become a symbol for the pilots who flew for Eastern, and for all of its employees.

But there were other "Aces" like Raoul Lufbery, Douglas Campbell, and many more American fliers, well known at that time.

The most famous fighter aircraft that flew against the German Air Forces during WWI were the Nieuport 28 X111 fighter and the Spad X111. Some of the pilots who fought in the skies during that time said they believed the most realistic air-combat scenes ever made for a movie related to WWI were the dog fight scenes in the silent movie *Wings*. All those movies bit me hard.

During the late 1940s and early 1950s, when radio was still king, I listened to the Eastern Air Line commercials: "The Great Silver Fleet now is departing for—" Wherever the city was, it seemed far away and exciting. Every time I heard about Eastern Airlines or read about Rickenbacker, I knew I wanted to fly for Eastern Air Lines someday. I also realized that to pass an airline physical I had to be in tip-top shape.

If I read that most pilots chew their food on the left side of their mouths, I would chew my food on the left side. If I heard they exercise lifting weights, doing sit-ups, and push-ups, I would do the same.

I learned there were other requirements. Your eyesight had to be 20/20 without glasses. I had that one nailed. However, I read one way to improve your eyesight was with a pencil. You focus your eyes on the point, then follow it as you move it up, down, and sideways. You then bring it to your nose until your eyes cross. You repeat this exercise for at least ten minutes. Even though it sounds crazy, I did it every chance I got. Did it work? I believe it did.

One of my closest friends, Gene Horton, had the same interest I had in flying. (Years later, he became an exceptionally talented art teacher for one of the local high schools.) As seniors, we both began dating. Gene's girl was Judy Young, a very attractive Sophomore, and one of the football team's cheerleaders. She always seemed to be full of vigor. I, at the time, was dating no one, that is until I met Barbara Jean Johnson, who was also a Sophomore, and a football cheerleader full of vigor.

I met Barbara while standing in line at the school cafeteria. I was buying a small carton of milk for lunch and was a couple of cents short. She happened to be standing right behind me in her cheerleader's uniform. I turned around and asked her if she could loan me two cents, telling her I would pay her back. Of course, I thought this very beautiful girl would say no. She was the sister of one of my classmates, although I didn't know her. In her senior year, she was voted the girl with the nicest smile in her class. (My brother Glenn was voted nicest boy smile.) To my surprise, she lent me the two cents. After that, it seemed that every time I walked down a hallway or turned a corner in school, she would be there. It was shortly after a couple of these "bump-in meetings" that we started dating.

Interestingly, Judy's father was a pilot and a licensed aircraft mechanic. I met him one night when Gene and I went out on a double date. Les Young was one of those gentlemen that came from the old school of fliers during the 1920s, 1930s, 1940s, and 1950s. He worked for Atlantic Aviation at Teterboro Airport as an aircraft mechanic and knew many of the famous "barnstormers" who made early aviation history. Amelia Earhart, Jimmy Doolittle, and Arthur Godfrey were just a few of the famous flyers he spoke about. In his off time, Les would repair airplanes that people damaged or those that needed FAA-required maintenance checks. When he found out about my interest in aviation, he invited me to help repair some of the wrecks. No pay—which my dad wasn't happy about—but for me, it was the opportunity of a lifetime. Just to be able to sit in the cockpit of a busted-up Cessna or Piper aircraft was an amazing experience. I could hold the controls, gaze at the instrument panels, the altimeters, airspeed indicators, and tachometers, and imagine myself flying.

Under Les's guidance, I learned how to repair a damaged wing or fuselage by cutting and bending aluminum and then riveting it to the body of the plane. Some of the damaged aircraft were made of wood and fabric and repairing them required sewing and was more tedious. The smell of aircraft lacquer could be overwhelming and we would only do these repairs in an open environment. We had to spread the fabric over the airframe and then apply dope or lacquer to it. This would stiffen the fabric and make the wings airtight and weatherproof.

On several occasions, Les would let me come along when he did mainte-nance flight checks, required after the repair work was completed. He could only fly the plane with the owner's permission, which they always seemed to grant.

My first airplane ride was in a 1947 four-place Stinson Voyager tail-dragger that was built by the Consolidated Vultee Aircraft Company. Its frame was constructed of steel tubing and covered with fabric. A 165-horse-power Franklin engine propelled it through the skies. Les and the owner were in the process of checking the reliability of an altimeter that he replaced. As we flew along, Les kidded me by asking me if I knew where we were, knowing I had never been up in an airplane before. I surprised him when I was able to tell him the names of the towns and roadways as we flew over them. I think it was because my parents had driven the same countryside many times with us kids in the car, pointing out sights that they thought would be interesting. After that flight, I was truly bitten by the flying bug.

Soon after that, Gene and I decided to take flying lessons out of Hack-ettstown Airport, eighteen miles from where we lived. We learned it would cost $8.00 an hour if we did it as a duo, which meant with a flight instructor. To do it solo was $6.00 an hour. Either way, it was a lot of money in 1953.

Hackettstown Airport then, and still, is a country-style airport. Located in the rolling hills of beautiful Warren County, it featured two short grass strip runways. There was no control tower, only a few hangars, cornfields on the approaches, with cows and horses grazing in nearby meadows. But to me, this was the real deal. Gene and I were going to become barnstorming pilots, like in the movies.

I knew my parents would not let me take flying lessons, much less pay for them, even though I had been helping Les Young. But my ambition to fly was greater than ever. Somehow, I had to find a way to get permission from my parents to let the flight instructor we had already talked to, unbeknownst to my parents, teach me to fly. I would also need money to pay for the flying lessons.

11

WINGING IT

I had to fly and that meant I needed money for lessons. Mom was still putting fifty-cent pieces into her tin can, but I wasn't going there. I had learned my lesson about that one the hard way. But, without my parents' knowledge, accepting that I wasn't going to be another Harry James or Elvis Presley, I went to a pawn shop and sold my trumpet and guitar to pay for my first flying lessons. Later, I would use whatever I earned from my newspaper route, tips, which were few and far between, and some money I saved from working at the meat market. But there was still a big problem: How to get my parents' permission.

I knew my parents would not sign the required papers. I had no choice. I had to find someone who would be willing to forge one of my parents' names onto the waiver form that would allow me to take the lessons. The question was who. A sudden brainstorm hit.

Gene's mother, Vi, who I had known growing up, and who knew my parents, had signed his waiver. Would she sign mine?

After an hour of Gene and me begging, along with our assurances that we wouldn't "crack up," she finally reluctantly forged my mom's name on my waiver. To this day, I do not know if she contacted my parents for their permission. I believe she did, but I never asked. Why ruin the mystery? But, at least the form was signed.

The next step was the required FAA physical. This had to be done by a certified aviation doctor before I could solo an aircraft. Gene and I made great haste to visit the doctor. When we got to his office, it suddenly dawned on me that I might need my parent's permission to take the exam.

Fortunately, the doctor didn't ask for that. All went well. The exercises I had been performing must have helped. My vision was charted as 20/15, and I passed all phases of the exam—pardon the pun—with flying colors. The doctor signed the necessary documents that showed we passed our Third-Class Medical Examination.

In the Autumn of 1953, with those forms in hand, we began our first day of flight instruction. Gene was seventeen and I was sixteen years of age. The sky was getting nearer.

Our first flight instructor was Joe Schwanda, the owner of the airport. The aircraft we would learn on was a yellow Piper J-3 Cub with a 65-horsepower Continental Engine, registration number N70304. Seeing it reminded me of that day when I first looked skyward and saw one just like it soaring overhead.

The first thing Joe taught us about flying was, "you fly by the seat of your pants." That meant, you fly by the feel of THE PLANE: the amount of pressure you apply to the joystick, the ailerons, elevator, rudder, and what you see. A pilot needs to feel things that he may not get from his instruments. Ask any pilot and they will tell you about that feeling you have in the seat of your pants when you know you are about to make a hard landing. You have this involuntary urge to want to get your butt off the seat. The only trouble is that the seat belt keeps you from doing so and you get to feel the result…really, really, hard.

The first couple of lessons were sporadic due to bad weather and my being low on funds. I had to work every night after school and on Saturdays to try and pay for my lessons. After a few more lessons, our flying came to a halt.

However, none of those flights were ever logged or signed by Joe showing our flight time. He would tell us another flight instructor named Ernie Billows would do the signing. Which Ernie eventually did.

Joe's son, Donnie, was older than Gene and I were. He had a commercial pilot's license, and on occasion, would fly with us when Joe wasn't available.

Many years later, he would take over the airport and its operation after his father died. Strangely enough, Donnie would become our sons, Scott and Keith's, flight instructor twenty-five years after my first flying lesson with his father. Both of my sons would become Air Force Pilots and fly combat missions. Scott would fly RC-135s in "Operation Desert Storm," the Iraq war. Keith flew Lockheed's C-130 Hercules during the Bosnian War, Iraqi Freedom, and in Afghanistan. Both would receive Air Medals. Today, both are airline pilots. Scott is a United Air Lines Captain; Keith is a Southwest Air Lines Captain. I guess flying is in our genes.

But way back then, driving to the airport from Dover for a one-hour flying lesson was a challenge. If Gene or I drove, when my parents let me borrow their car, still not knowing I was taking flying lessons, it came down to who could drive to the airport the quickest. To make our appointments, we drove with reckless abandon, not caring too much about the cars we passed on the two-lane roads we raced down. It was always, "pedal to the metal," and, "Damn the torpedoes! Full speed ahead!" I think I still own the record.

After the flying lessons, at Gene's or our home, we would sit on a chair in the kitchen, or in the basement, pretending we were in the cockpit of that tandem two-seat J-3 Cub, and practice our lessons. When I was home, when my parents weren't around, it was: grab the toilet plunger, the kind with the rubber suction cup and a wooden handle, which looked similar to the joystick of the J-3 Cub. I'd sit in a chair, stick the plunger to the floor, and grab this imaginary joystick in my right hand. With my left hand, I'd grasp an imaginary throttle in the same position it would be on the left side of the cockpit of the J-3. I don't know how many hours that chair and I did doing take-offs and landings, forced landings, stalls, s-turns over a road, circles of 360 or 720-degree turns, and missed approaches. But for each practice session, I would move both feet and my hands as though I was really at the controls.

And it wasn't just the fun and adventure of flying. During those flying lessons, I was reading a book Les Young gave me, entitled *Stick and Rudder* by Wolfgang Langewiesche. His book went into detail about the aerodynamics of flight and the science of flying. He described what made an aircraft stall, the angle of attack, the p-factor of the propeller, flight controls, and recovering from a spin. I was fascinated as he discussed the weight and balance of the aircraft and the effect of g-loads which put stress on the wings, airframe, and body of the plane. I studied the requirements of aircraft maintenance logbooks, etcetera. I wanted to learn it all. It was all invaluable to me. Years later, as a flight instructor, I used Langewiesche's ideas and knowledge to help teach others to fly. Now that I knew what I wanted to do, I would let nothing stop me.

12

CAR TROUBLE

I had taken several more lessons after my first solo and came home each day from the airport believing my parents still didn't know what I was up to.

Suddenly, one day, when I walked through the door, the first thing my dad said was, "How are the flying lessons going?"

I thought my heart stopped beating for a moment. I was in trouble again. My dream of flying was about to come crashing down.

My parents never told me how they found out about my lessons, and I wasn't going to ask them. At first, I thought it was my aunt who lived in Hackettstown, not far from the airport, who knew my secret and told my parents. But the more I thought about it, I didn't believe she did rat on me. Some of the kids going to high school with me knew. Some of the teachers found out, but not from me. Word gets around fast when you don't want it to. But, looking back on it now, I think Gene's mother was the one who spilled the beans. Anyway, my parents never let on that they knew, and I'm guessing they gave her the okay to sign my waiver form. Thank goodness.

My four years of high school, which seemed like forever, weren't without conflict. Before I entered high school, the Korean War, Korean Conflict as it was called, broke out on Sunday, June 6, 1950. Some of our seniors, seventeen and eighteen-year-old boys, had joined the Army National Guard before Korea. They were the first to be sent overseas and ended up on the front lines. Some were killed in combat, including PFC Donald J. Kearney, who lived a couple of blocks away. When people die in combat, it's a war, not a police action as the politicians claimed.

The war continued until July 27, 1953, when both sides agreed to an armistice. Technically, even today, there is no peace treaty and it's still only a ceasefire.

As I was nearing the end of my four years of high school, only a month from graduating, I looked forward to what lay ahead. We all knew we would have just three choices: go on to college, be drafted, or join a branch of the military, with or without a war going on. I had little interest in academics, which ruled out college. That meant I would be military-bound. I was still determined to become an airline pilot but knew there were obstacles in my path.

Our guidance counselor, Dale Weaver, was very helpful. He pointed out the Navy had a program for pilots called The Naval Aviation Cadet Program, NavCad. He explained their requirements were high and rightly so. You had to have a college degree, pass exams, and their physicals. If you qualified, you were obligated to serve active duty for five to six years. I knew I did not want to spend that many years in the military. There was a second option. The navy offered a program called the "Kiddy-Cruise." If you joined before your eighteenth birthday, the Navy would discharge you on your 21st birthday, and, you would be entitled to receive the Korean G.I. Bill. The bill entitled you to receive money towards the college of your choice. I picked "door" number two.

But before graduating I managed to get myself into more trouble. Several more times.

The first incident happened because I didn't have an automobile of my own. On occasion, my dad would allow me to drive his 1952 Mercury to school and afterward drive it to work. One morning the weather was warm and clear. Some friends that I hung around with piled into the car and we started off for Dover High School. By the time we arrived, and after driving around the high school several times looking for a parking place, with none to be found, I opted for choice number two.

It was a good day to play hooky. I drove to Pennsylvania and we took in the sights. I made sure we would be back by the time school let out. After dropping my friends off at their homes, I drove to work. It was a fun day and none of us were going to get caught. The following day, we each wrote a note stating we were sick. We signed our parents' names to them.

Unfortunately, some teachers saw us driving around the school that morning. Dumb. I was called into Vice-Principal Herbert Spurway's office and was told we were seen driving around the high school. He said he knew the names of all the guys involved except one.

He asked me who the student was.

I told Vice-Principal Spurway I wasn't going to tell him.

That's when he said, "In that case, because it was your car and you were driving, the school is going to press kidnapping charges against you because you took these minors across the state line into Pennsylvania."

"Kidnapping!" My mind went blank. I had no choice. Without hesitation, I told him what he wanted to know. The odd thing about it was that all of the kids with me that day had to have their parents come to the school except mine.

To this day, the person whose name I had to reveal still reminds me of that day. Today, we laugh about it. But that day, I was terrified I had crashed my entire future with a dumb "joyride."

Mr. Spurway, the Vice-Principal, was also one of my teachers in high school who I liked. I was always very respectful to him. For whatever reason, he never called my parents about what I did. And I wasn't about to tell them.

One thing I do have to mention about Mr. Spurway was his remarkable courage. Someone told me that as a kid he used to hop freight trains as a lark until he slipped and fell off a moving train. Both his hands were severed by the train's steel wheels. After the terrible accident and many months of recovery, he was fitted with prosthetic steel claws. There were a couple of occasions when he would be demonstrating something to our class and shake his hand vigorously emphasizing his point. Off would come the hand and fly through the air. We'd duck as it whizzed past. He would calmly walk over to where his hand lay, pick it up, set it aside on his desk and continue his lecture. After class, he would take it down to the machine shop and get it re-attached. I admired him but was surprised he never told my parents what I did. Maybe, he was a bit of a daredevil too.

There was another incident. Dad's "52" Mercury, I found out, was a fast car.

Late one night while alone, I decided to do a speed run just to see how fast the car could go. I drove from the intersection of Route 10 and Dover Chester Road to the intersection of Route 10 and Canfield Avenue two miles away. Assuring myself there was no traffic or police, and that the highway was clear of debris, I slammed on the pedal. I pegged out the speedometer at over 120 miles per hour. 120 was the most the speedometer showed. I then proceeded to do the same thing in the opposite direction. My dad never could figure out why the car was burning oil.

And then there was the evening I had to outrun a Randolph police car.

That night I had some of the guys with me. I was driving eastbound on Route 10 and going about ten miles per hour over the speed limit. Suddenly, I saw a police car coming in the opposite direction. The next thing I noticed was his red lights flashing as he passed me. He turned around, crossed over the median, and began chasing me.

Like an idiot, I began to try to outrun him. I stomped down on the gas pedal and accelerated to 90 miles an hour, then did a high-speed turn off the highway onto a back road, blowing the horn to pass cars ahead of me and barely missing oncoming cars. I heard his siren and looked in the rear-view mirror. He was catching up. The only thing I could think about was what was going to happen when my dad finds out about this if I'm caught.

Luckily, we came to a curve in the road where we couldn't see the police car and he couldn't see me. I jammed on the brakes, turned into someone's walled driveway, killed the engine, turned off the headlights, and we all ducked down.

Seconds later the cruiser came whizzing by, siren wailing. Suddenly the owner of the home turned on his porch lights. I threw the car into reverse, and with tires squealing backed out and drove the speed limit all the way home.

Luckily, my parents never knew about my race with the police car. But guys can't keep from talking. By the end of the week, some of my teachers were asking me, "How fast does a Mercury Automobile go?" The cop I was fortunate to escape from was Chief Okum. He was known as a real tough Randolph policeman. In my yearbook, they printed a caption about me that read, "A Hot Rod Car and A Dollar Bill, He's One of The Boys from Thompson Hill." The dollar bill came from a bet I made with Barbara's brother, Eddie, that he wouldn't kiss a certain female schoolmate. Which he did.

It was not long after the police chase incident, even though nothing was ever said about it, that my Dad's car became "off-limits." I was told I wasn't going to drive it for a long while. That's when I came up with another no-fail idea.

13

A CAR CALLED BIG AL

Two of the guys I hung around with were Bill Brown and Bobby Scales. We came up with the bright idea of buying a 1936 four-door Dodge Touring Car that would only cost us 35 dollars. We would not let our parents know we bought the car. Great plan.

It was a great car. Black, with two sidewall tires mounted on the front fenders, it looked like the type of gangster car you would see in the movies, which is why I named it "Big Al," after Al Capone. Bill and Bobby chipped in ten dollars apiece and I put in fifteen. Because I put in the most money, the car was in my name.

I would park the car a couple of blocks from where we lived so my parents wouldn't see it. When they left for work, I would go get the car, pick up the guys on the way to school, and we would take turns driving it.

Several weeks later, my parents found out about the car. They were really mad. Not so much for me not telling them I had it, but because there was no insurance on it. The following day, we insured it. I had to help pay for it. Honestly, I was surprised they let me keep it.

It was a great car, but had one bad habit.

Once in a while, it would let out a loud backfire. One night, around eleven o'clock, I happened to be on Blackwell Street, the main street in Dover. I was taking Gene home when the car let out a loud backfire. The next thing we know, a police car, its tires screeching and siren wailing came racing around the corner and pulled us over. Two police officers jumped out of the car with their guns drawn. When they realized my car had back-fired, and it was not gunfire, they put their guns away and told us to get home. The problem was that "Al" could still shoot out a loud backfire at any time.

Gene lived about three miles from where we were. The question was how to get him home without the possibility of more backfires being mistaken for gun blasts.

I realized that the car never backfired when driven in reverse. Another brilliant idea! I decided to drive in reverse to Gene's home. Which we did.

Primarily, because there was no traffic at that time of night, and we were on backcountry roads, driving backwards did the trick and I got Gene home without more cops showing up with guns drawn.

After I dropped Gene off, I drove another two miles in reverse to our home. I would have laughed but having a car sound like gunshots was a big problem. Several days later, one of the guys who knew about engine timing fixed the car and thankfully, it never backfired again.

Shortly before my parents knew I had the car, Scales, Brown, and I had another brilliant idea. We drove it to Newark, New Jersey, which was about thirty miles away. The attraction? Minsky's Burlesque. We wanted to see what some of the older guys were raving about.

The Empire Theater opened in 1912 and was located on Washington Street in Newark. In its heyday, many famous strippers performed there. Lili St. Cyr had her bath routine while Rosita Royce had trained doves. Georgia Sothern was known as the fiery redhead and used fire as part of her routine. There were also comedians. Forget the comedians, we were going to see the strippers. Of course, we did not tell our parents.

At first, the management wasn't going to allow us in because of our ages. I was only seventeen. But for some reason, they let us stand in the back of the theater. It was a very long, long way from the stage, but we were all excited to see our first strip show.

My first impression of the strippers we saw was, "God, do they look old." The women were wearing a lot of lipstick and went heavy on the rouge. I don't think we stayed much more than an hour before we left. I still remember their acts. At the time, I thought the comedians were better. At the time.

One afternoon, while I was driving down Blackwell Street, the main street in Dover, I was rear-ended by another car. My car was built like a tank and had no damage. I asked the woman who hit me if she was alright. She said she was. Her car had a good size dent in its front grill, but she told me not to worry about it. I wasn't. After all, she hit me. We both got back in our cars and drove off.

When I told my dad what happened, he asked me if I got the woman's name and address. Did I check her driver's license and her car insurance? All of which I answered, no. He wasn't too happy about that.

The following day, I went to the site where the accident occurred, at the intersection next to Louis's Market. It just so happened that my car was pointing in the same direction as when I was rear-ended. For whatever reason, I started driving not knowing where I was going. It was as if I was being guided by some unseen force. I continued down Blackwell Street, rounded Dead Man's Curve, which borders the town of Rockaway, drove to Route 46, turned right, drove several more miles, turned left at the traffic light on Franklin Road, looked to my right, and there was the car that hit me. It was parked in a driveway over seven miles from where she hit my car. I drove home and told my dad I had found the car.

He said, "Don't worry about it."

What puzzled me was the fact that I had no idea where she lived yet found her car. Was it just luck? ESP? Guardian Angels? I've often wondered about that incident and others that happened in my life.

14

GOODBYE HIGH SCHOOL

D over, at that time, was a thriving community. Friday nights, on Blackwell Street, you would often see teenagers cruising up and down the street in their souped-up cars. With car rear-ends lowered, and mufflers rumbling, guys would be looking to pick up girls. That would go on until the stores closed for the night. There was another reason people would flock to our town on Friday nights: The Dover Speedway.

The speedway was well recognized throughout the stock-car racing circuit. It opened on June 11, 1933, and closed down in 1935. It then returned and ran from 1947 through 1952 and closed down again. It re-opened and operated from June 12, 1954, to July 10, 1954.

The racetrack featured sprint and stock-car racing around a banked quarter-mile oil-dirt track. The stock cars were of the 1940s and early 1950s vintage. Their drivers would race at break-neck speed to capture first place with the hope of winning hundreds of dollars awarded for each race.

The racetrack was operating for less than one month when on the night of July 10, 1954, I was there. I watched the last car in a race making a terrific challenge, coming from behind to overtake the leader. As he rounded the third turn, he lost control of his car. It went up the side of the bank, hit the short-rail fence, and flipped over it upside-down. Everyone in the stands stood up to see what happened. When we did, the center section of the stands collapsed.

Luckily, I was standing on the edge of the first set of the three sets of stands right next to those that collapsed. It was as though someone pulled out the rug beneath the victims' feet. There was a lot of screaming from the injured who suffered broken bones and were still trapped between the seats.

Fortunately, during the races, the fire department and rescue squad were always standing by in the event of a stock car accident and reacted immediately. But a lot of people went to the hospital that night. It was later presumed that the g-force of so many people standing up at once placed too much downward pressure on the stands, the possible reason they collapsed. A lot of lawsuits were filed because of the accident. And that was the end of the Dover Speedway.

Had I been standing another couple of inches to my left I would have gone down with them. Another lucky break or guardian angel?

An ugly incident I will always remember happened while I was still a senior, during the school's basketball season. Our high school was playing a team from a neighboring community. As usual when the first period ended, during the break, I hustled over to "Dicks Diner," next to the high school to grab a cup of coffee. As I came out of the diner, I noticed several classmates of mine who were on the varsity football team, standing around. They were waiting for several guys from the community that we were playing against to come out of the diner. Apparently, heated words were exchanged during the first period, and now these guys were bent on vengeance.

As each one from the other town came out, one of my classmates would grab him by the front of his shirt and ask our football players, "Is this the guy?" The answer was no. Then the last kid came out. He was the shortest of all of them. One of our players yelled, "That's the guy!" What happened next was repulsive. My two classmates, who instigated the confrontation, started hitting this short kid. He managed to break free and began running down the street, trying to get away. All of us who witnessed the beating, as though we were caught in a whirlwind, or a cattle stampede, chased him down the street.

My classmate tackled the kid in the middle of the road. He pushed his face into the pavement, grabbed his left arm, yanked it behind his back, and pushed it upwards until he broke it.

When that happened, we all ran, leaving that poor kid in the middle of the road.

The following Monday, our principal made an announcement over the school's intercom asking for anyone with information about the incident to come forward. No one did, including me. From that moment on, the other high school vowed never to play our school again in any sport, and they kept that promise. I will never forget that incident, nor those players who were responsible, and the person who broke the kid's arm. I will also never forget my not coming forward.

Graduation from high school came and went. Barbara and I agreed it would be best for both of us to put our relationship on hold. She, being a Sophomore, had two more years of high school before she graduated. For me, it would be the navy's recruiting poster that beckoned: "Join the Navy and See the World."

But before that...

On August 22, 1954, after nine hours of flying lessons, the day finally came when Gene and I made our first solo flight in the J-3. I was singing from the time I took off to the time I touched down. No one can understand the tremendous feeling of accomplishment when you first solo an airplane unless they have done it themselves.

My joy was short-lived.

"Uncle Sam wants you!"

15

HELLO NAVY

On September 16, 1954, my parents brought me to the naval induction center in New York City. There, I raised my right hand and was sworn into the United States Navy, pledging to protect the United States from all its enemies. I was now the property of Uncle Sam.

Up until that time, I always thought my dad was strict. Forget that. No sooner had I, and those being inducted with me sworn in, when we quickly found out there was a higher authority than our parents, and that was a Chief Boatswain Mate. He barked more orders in one breath than I ever thought possible. "Oh, oh, what did I get myself into now?"

By the time I enlisted, the Korean Conflict, War, was over. Although we were supposedly at peace, there were still swords rattling between China and Taiwan, once called Formosa, an island nation not far from the coast of China. President Harry S. Truman dispatched the US Navy's 7th Fleet into the Taiwan Strait to prevent hostilities between Taiwan and the China mainland. Tensions were high as I said goodbye to New York and hello to the Navy's basic training center (boot camp) in Bainbridge, Maryland for nine weeks. The camp was named after Commodore William Bainbridge, noted for his many victories at sea during the 1800s, and once the Commander of the U.S.S. Constitution.

My military training commenced with learning about ordnance, and simulated gunnery practice. Seamanship and firefighting were also at the top of the list. All of the programs were set up as though all of us were to be assigned to shipboard duty. We all took a series of exams to evaluate what trades we were most suited for before being assigned to the fleet. What did they have in mind for me? That would be a surprise.

Nighttime in the barracks was an adventure. For those of us who have never lived in a barracks with 89 guys, who came from the North, South, East, and West, it was, well, an experience. I never knew so many young men snored. Think of 89 buzz saws all running at the same time.

At first, trying to get to sleep with all that racket was nearly impossible. It proves you can get used to almost anything.

The Navy was pushing to man its ships, and what was supposed to be nine weeks of basic training was cut down to six weeks. Marching, calisthenics, firefighting, learning how to enter smoke-filled rooms the proper way, handling of hazardous material, jumping off the side of a platform into water to simulate abandoning ship, guard duty requirements, saluting officers the proper way, and a ton of classroom studies seemed to be crammed into one day. It wasn't long before I slept like a log. Close your eyes for a moment, and just like that, Reveille.

There were two groups that I remember the most while I was in Bainbridge. One was a group of six guys from the streets of New York City who had all been part of the same gang, so they said. They reminded me of the movie *Angels with Dirty Faces*. Initially, they tried to intimidate some of us with their tough street talk. After a few scuffles, that idea was quickly quashed.

The other group was ten guys from Scranton, Pennsylvania, many with the same last name, Kelly. None of them were related. I would chum around with them while I was there.

During the many days of taking the aptitude written exams, I requested to be placed with naval aviation. After the exams, the Navy thought I should be an Aviation Storekeeper, dealing with aircraft supplies. They wanted to send me to Norman, Oklahoma, for training. After several months of schooling, I would be sent to a fleet as a supply clerk. The Navy had dozens of fleets.

I replied that I didn't want to be a clerk and asked them to give me something like aircraft maintenance. I explained that I had some aircraft maintenance background while helping Les Young. They told me they would see what they could do.

Graduation came, not cap and gown, ala high school, but in a sailor uniform.

All through our basic training, the rumor mill had it that it would be "Destination Taiwan" for most of us after we completed boot camp.

I was hoping for an aircraft carrier like the boys from Scranton, Pennsylvania got. They were assigned to the aircraft carrier USS. Antietam. Several of the "Dead End Kids" were assigned to the Brooklyn Navy Yard. The rest of us were scattered to the four winds. The good news: none of us were going to Taiwan.

For me, it was goodbye Bainbridge, hello Naval Air Station Brunswick, Maine.

I was lucky to be a land sailor.

16

FIRST ASSIGNMENT

I was assigned to VP-11, a Naval Anti-Submarine Air Patrol Squadron that flew Lockheed's P2V-5 Neptunes. The trek to get there was taking a train from Baltimore to New York's Grand Central Station. Then hop on another train ride to Boston and switch to another train to Portland, Maine. From there, I had to take the Boston Maine Railroad to Brunswick. I arrived just before the first snowfall of winter.

My uniform sleeve no longer bore the patch with the two white stripes indicating you were a boot recruit. Instead, I was wearing three green stripes that specified I was an airman—a raw airman, but an airman. However, my orders did not indicate exactly what I would be trained to do in the squadron. I was still hoping to become an aircraft mechanic through the Navy's on-the-job training.

But first came the indoctrination of the squadron's history that started with Catalina PBYs, two-engine patrol aircraft. I learned that during World War II, the squadron flew many night combat missions in the South Pacific and became known as the "Black Cats." They had a remarkable World War II battle record. After the war ended, the squadron was relocated to Quonset Point, Rhode Island. The Consolidated Vultee PB4Y-2's Privateer replaced the PBY. Years later, the latter would be replaced with Lockheed's P2V-5s and the squadron would be relocated to Brunswick, Maine several months before I joined them. Unfortunately, in the summer of 1954, one of the squadron's P2s went down in Bermuda's Harbor with loss of life. There was always that risk.

Once away from the rigid boot camp training I had experienced at Bainbridge, the Squadron was a surprise. I was now regular Navy, which meant you mustered at 8 a.m., worked eight hours, then were on your own time. And, we had weekends off. Hello, liberty. Still, you would have to do guard duty for four hours, mostly guarding aircraft.

Our sleeping quarters were also a nice surprise compared to the barracks in Bainbridge. We were housed in one of the many buildings used for enlisted men. We still had bunk beds, but there were only four men in a cubicle. Each of the three levels in the building held eighty men. It didn't matter what your rank was. Whether you were an Airman like me, right on up to First Class Petty Officer, you were in the same building. Thanks to those walled cubicles, the snoring level was cut down drastically. There was also a quiet area on the main floor that had a television, writing desks, sofa, cushioned chairs, and assorted magazines for our enjoyment. Quite a change from boot camp.

One thing that impressed me was that you never had to go outside to get to the mess hall. Each building was connected by an enclosed walkway. When it rained, sleeted, or snowed—and it snowed in feet, not inches—you could walk to the mess in casual clothing.

While in high school, I made it a point to use the school library reference books to search for information, not only about aviation but about our Dover's history. This honed my interest in the history of the places where I was stationed.

There were two picturesque towns nearby where I would spend most of my time. Brunswick and Bath Maine were interesting places. Brunswick was a small scenic town at the time, not far from Maine's rugged coastline. The town's main income came from the thousands of Navy personnel based there, so we were always welcomed with open arms. Its most notable historic site was Bowdoin College, where, by the way, I once took voice lessons with the idea of becoming a singer in the entertainment world. But only if I couldn't become an airline pilot.

Bowdoin was also the college that Joshua Chamberlain attended long before he became famous during the Battle of Gettysburg. As a Lieutenant Colonel, he commanded the Union Armies' 20th Maine Regiment during the Battle of Little Round Top. For his valor and command leadership, he was awarded the Medal of Honor. He later became president of the college and then the Governor of Maine. Our squadron had a Lt. Chamberlain who commanded one of our P2s. I was told he was a descendant of Joshua Chamberlain and I never did ask him.

Just a stone's throw from Brunswick lies Bath, Maine, which sits on the Kennebec River. It had its history of Indians called the Abenakis but was most noted for The Bath Iron Works, builder of our navy's destroyers. During World War II, the ironworks averaged one destroyer every seventeen days, an amazing feat during that time.

The navy employs specific designations to identify the different types of naval aircraft squadrons. The V, for example, stands for heavier than air. VP, for patrol. VF for fighters. VR, for transports. VH, for helicopters, and ZP, for lighter-than-air vehicles, such as blimps.

VP-11, like all combat units, had its logo, The Proud Pegasus, a white stallion with wings and a lightning bolt in the background. On its horizontal stabilizer (vertical fin) were the large blocked letters, HB, denoting the squadron's identification.

Here I was, a green wet-behind-the-ears seventeen-year-old, now part of a combat-ready patrol squadron that could hunt down enemy submarines and warships in times of war. My first reaction to seeing these mighty patrol bombers parked on the ramp was awe. They were beautiful, and big when compared to the J-3 Piper Cub I had flown. They were graceful looking except the plane looked as though it was eight-and-a-half months pregnant. Its pregnant appearance came from the APS-20 radar mounted in its underbelly, just aft of the nose wheel, and ready to detect surface vessels. The plane carried ASW/ECM (Anti-Submarine Warfare/Electronic Counter Measures) equipment. But it was the stinger in its tail that mattered the most for it housed the MAD (Magnetic Anomaly Detection) system, which was the equipment used to detect submarines, ours and the enemy's.

In simple terms, a submerged submarine creates an anomaly in the earth's magnetic field. Our aircraft would drop sonobuoys in a set pattern across many miles of ocean. These floating devices were outfitted with listening systems about the size of a fence post and would release a string of microphones hundreds of feet in length underwater.

When a submarine was detected, the MAD electronics technician who monitors the search would yell out, "MAD, MAD, MAD!" This indicated to the crew he had a submarine contact and would call out the direction and distance for a possible intercept.

The P2 was also capable of dropping mines, bombs, torpedoes, and depth charges, and could even fire rockets from under its wings. It carried a .50 caliber machine gun placed forward of the horizontal stabilizer.

Wingtip fuel tanks allowed for longer missions, some of which could last for more than twelve hours. The plane also had a one million candle-power searchlight on its right-wing tip for night hunting.

For me, the big attraction to the P2 was its plexiglass nose cone designed for maximum observation. The observer would sit in the cone's bucket seat and have 180 degrees of unobstructed visibility. The nose was also used to take photographs during missions. Our squadron had twelve P2V-5s that were powered by two Wright Cyclone R-3350 engines. Later, they were replaced by the newer P2V-7 models. Lockheed had added two J-34 jet engines. I was happy to be part of this squadron. Soon, I thought, I would be working on aircraft engines, a big step toward my dream.

Then came the wake-up call.

17

SAVED BY A TYPEWRITER

"Report to the Chief Boatswain Mate's office."

The office was a small duty shack located on the main hangar deck. My first thought was what the heck is a Chief Boatswain Mate doing in an aircraft patrol squadron? He's regular navy. Isn't he supposed to be on a ship somewhere?

When I reported, the Chief informed me that I would be working for him until they either sent me to work in the mess hall for two weeks, or do compartment cleaning (barracks) for two weeks, or both until they decided what to do with me. Not good in any case.

I worked in that cubbyhole for several days, doing odd jobs, while the navy was making up its mind about what to do with me. After the third day, the Chief asked if I could type. I told him I took typing in high school.

"Fine. I want you to type a couple of letters for me, and by the way, you're going to be working in the mess hall at the end of the week."

A storm cloud of gloom was on the horizon. Was I never going to reach my dream?

A few days later, as luck would have it, the telephone rang while I was pounding away on the keys of my typewriter harder than I normally would. Dishing out food and being stuck in the mess was on my mind and my Underwood was taking the punishment.

The call was from the Chief in charge of supplies. He heard me pounding that typewriter over the telephone while he was talking to the Chief Boatswain Mate. Shortly after the call, he came down from his office, upstairs in the hangar, wanting to talk to my Chief. My chief explained that I was headed for duty in the mess hall. The Supply chief offered another option.

After some discussion, my Chief approached and asked if I wanted to work in the supply department or the mess hall, and later do compartment cleaning.

The choice was a no-brainer. I chose option number one. It seemed the supply department was going to be short one man because his enlistment was up after the squadron's next deployment, so they needed a replacement who could type.

I was now on course to become an Aviation Storekeeper by way of on-the-job training. Ironically, it was the same job the navy wanted to train me for after boot camp.

At first, my new assignment was a little confusing, but my mentor, Ray Beyers, the "short-timer", helped me. Before long, I got the hang of it. I ordered supplies for the aircraft and the squadron's needs: engines, spark plugs, replacement parts, pens, pencils, toilet paper, parachutes, flight suits, etcetera, etcetera, etcetera. "Fill out a stub requisition, type in the replacement nomenclature, how many, and the part number." Yes, even toilet paper had a part number. Then at the bottom of the stub requisition, I would type in the supply officer's rank and name followed by my initials. How well I remember. Lt. J.B. Klockenkemper, USN/RAF. Over the three years I served there, I must have typed thousands of stubs requisitions for different supply officers.

Once settled in, I was meeting new shipmates. Shortly after I arrived, three new men were also assigned to the squadron. Each had washed out of the NavCad flight training program in Pensacola, Florida. Now they were just plain airmen. One of them, a fellow named Altmier, from the west coast, seemed to adjust to being an enlisted man rather quickly. On occasion, we would go and see some of the local sights. The other two? Not so much. One thought he was an officer until one day one of the Chiefs set him straight. He and the third man had a hard time adjusting to being enlisted men.

One day Alt and I heard there was a carnival in town setting up tents and rides for the grand opening. We decided to check it out the night before it opened. Because our workday ended around 5 p. m. we arrived late in the evening. All the tents were up, as were the rides. Some townspeople were milling around. Several appeared to be farmers wearing bib overalls. One tent had a lot of men gathered inside. We decided to see what the attraction was.

A stage had been set up for exotic dancers. Women were dancing, wearing Hawaiian-style grass hula skirts. They did a short performance, then disappeared behind the curtain. About four minutes later, they returned to the stage without their hula skirts. They were stark naked from the waist down. The lights in the tent suddenly went out and it was pitch black. As if on cue, about a dozen or more flashlights, many from the guys who were wearing those overalls, lit up the stage as though it was a yearly event. Those that were standing next to the stage were invited to…let's just say I got an education that night. Yes, we did go back on opening night. It wasn't the same. The dancers kept their clothes on throughout their performance. A large disappointment.

Winters in Maine could be severe. It was worse when you had to pull guard duty. You were given a Colt .45 caliber handgun, a cartridge belt, and several clips, each holding seven rounds of ammunition. You were not allowed to load your weapon unless you came across someone about to sabotage an airplane. Of course, if there ever was a saboteur, most likely you'd be dead by the time you got your .45 out and began loading it. As a guard, you would walk the perimeter of the ramp checking the aircraft. You would do that circuit for four hours until you were relieved. The duty watch I normally got was from midnight to four in the morning and of course, when it was snowing. They did have an outside line shack for maintenance personnel where I could take a few moments to get warm, but then it was back outside. Occasionally, if the wind was blowing hard, it would cause white-out conditions. Still, I had to walk the perimeter, and that was dangerous, dodging snowplows. You could see them, but most of the time they couldn't see you.

Now and then, another problem was getting the guy who was to replace you out of his bunk, especially if he had the 4 a.m. to 8 a.m. duty. Our barracks had to have a guard on duty throughout the night, so one of his assignments was to wake the replacement a half-hour before he was due to go on watch. Most of the time, the replacement guards got right up. But there was always that one jerk who would just turn over and go back to sleep. Then the barracks guard would tell him he would have to get the duty officer. It always amazed me to see how quickly the jerk could get dressed and out the door. I guess the thought of time in the brig was a good persuader.

Our base had an Enlisted Men's Club. On Friday nights there would be entertainment of some sort. It was great for those who were married to be able to relax and enjoy the evening with their spouse. The single guys could bring a date. Some of these dates, as I found out, were called "ghosts." The ghosts would be the women who dated single guys in the squadron, either looking to get married or just out to have a good time. Whatever the reason, when the club closed, some of these couples would find a motel and spend the weekend there. Come Monday morning the women would disappear, hence the name "ghosts." They would reappear the next Friday night. I think it's reasonable to assume that all branches of the military had their ghosts. We did have one ghost who was well-known. We called her Radar because she would pick up any guy she could.

There were several other patrol squadrons besides VP-11 based at Brunswick. Notably, VP-8, VP-10, VP-23, and VP-26, but normally some of these squadrons were deployed for six months elsewhere. Some were stationed in Rota, Spain; Lajes, Azores; and Hal Far, Malta. My first deployment to Malta would come in April 1955, but before that, our squadron deployed to the Naval Air Station, Roosevelt Roads, in Puerto Rico. We stayed at "Rosy Roads" for two weeks, practicing naval maneuvers with the US Navy's 4th Fleet that cruised the Caribbean. While there, I was able to catch my first ride on one of the squadrons practicing rocket and bombing missions aboard the P2. It was almost my last.

18

MARTHA RAYE

A ccess to the P2 flight deck was either via a ladder that was located in the aft bulkhead of the nose wheel well or through a hatch located on the underbelly of the fuselage, just forward of the sonobuoy chutes. Getting into the observer's plexiglass nose dome while in flight was another matter. Once the nose wheel was retracted you had to squeeze through a narrow opening between the nose wheel and its bulkhead to get to the observer's seat. However, my first flight had me sitting in the after-station (back end) of the aircraft.

Once airborne, we flew toward our practice area, a small rocky island off the coast of Puerto Rico called Vieques, which was used as the bombing range. En route, an ensign and I poured ourselves a cup of coffee from the small galley. We then slipped over the wing root that separated the front of the aircraft from the back and eased past the technicians who would normally be using the ASW equipment to hunt subs. We began to make ourselves comfortable, sitting on the small canvas jump seats in the aft section of the aircraft.

As I sat down, the ensign latched both of the huge windows, on each side of the fuselage, open. The latch was on the top side of the window. We then put on our headsets to be able to hear the plane commander and to lessen the noise of air rushing past the open windows as we cruised along at approximately 180 mph. This being my first experience on a rocket run, the ensign stated the PC (plane commander) would start a shallow dive at the target, line it up, and then fire the rockets located underneath both wings. Neither of us put on our seat belts.

So, there I sat, fat, dumb, and happy, sipping coffee when the PC announced we were starting our rocket run. Suddenly, the P2 was thrust into a steep dive, and just as suddenly, the ensign and I were floating in space, a parabola (zero gravity), just like you see astronauts experience in their spacecraft. The tail-end of the plane was yawing back and forth as the commander worked the rudder pedals to keep fixed on the target. As the aircraft swayed, we began drifting to the left, toward the open window, my side.

There is no more helpless feeling than not being able to control your body. You claw for anything you can grab ahold of. All you come up with is empty air. Then comes that instant fear when you think you're about to be sucked out of the aircraft and hurled into space with no parachute and the Caribbean Sea waiting below. Just as I started to be sucked out of the plane, the commander reduced our dive angle. Gravity took over. The latch on the window released, catching me on the bridge of my nose. The ensign and I crashed down to the floor, blood streaming from my nose where the window hit it, coffee spilling over us. We both scrambled for our seats and strapped ourselves in, my heart pounding.

If the window had not been released, I most certainly would have been sucked out of the aircraft and would have become another accident statistic. The whole incident probably took no longer than twenty seconds. But a lesson was learned. Wear your seat belt. And give thanks to your Guardian Angels again.

Several days after my near-death experience, the squadron was treated to a visit by one of America's funniest ladies, Martha Raye. She and her troupe arrived in one of the Navy's R5-Ds, a Douglas DC-4. I can still remember her standing in the doorway of the cabin waving to everyone gathered to see her. She asked if any of us could help offload all their luggage. What a mad scramble that was. Guys pushed each other out of the way so that they could grab their bags, and at the same time try to get her autograph. What a performance she and her cast put on for us that night. For me, it was amazing that she and her troupe cared enough for guys like me and the others, to take the time—she had her television program then—to entertain troops outside of the United States. That was something I won't forget. Her unselfish acts of entertaining troops during World War II, Korea, and Vietnam earned her The Presidential Medal of Freedom presented by President Clinton on November 2, 1993. God bless her, and others like her, who entertained our troops during many years of war, sometimes putting their own lives at risk.

In April 1955, our squadron of P2s departed for Malta. Anyone who was not a flight crew member boarded R5Ds. This would be a two-day trip, with our first stop at Lajes, Azores. We were sitting on canvas seats attached to the side of the bulkheads, that were also used as sleeping cots. They made for a long uncomfortable flight. We were carrying cargo, mostly spare parts for the squadron's aircraft, which was the reason why the normal passenger seats were removed. Everything went smoothly until we were approaching Lajes when one of the flight crew members came out of the cockpit and announced in a loud voice, "We're going in."

19

MALTA

E very flyer fears the words, "We are going in." The passengers and I made frantic grabs for our Mae West Life Vests, thinking he meant we were about to ditch into the Atlantic Ocean. When the crewman realized what he had said, he quickly shouted, "No, no, no! We're going into land."

That correction was followed by many sighs of relief, including by me. Thankfully, it was a smooth landing.

I was looking forward to my first deployment, for two reasons. One, it would be my first time in a foreign country, and two, because of a movie I saw while in high school. It was called *The Malta Story* and starred Alec Guinness as a British fighter pilot who was based in Malta during World War II. What brought my attention to that movie and others like it were the playbills posted outside the movie theater. This poster showed Guinness standing near a fighter aircraft looking skyward as if searching for the enemy. The movie was about Royal Air Force pilots, their airplanes, and the brave people of Malta who endured heavy around-the-clock bombing raids by the Germans during WWII. I was impressed.

Malta is a small island of approximately 125 square miles located in the Mediterranean Sea, 50 miles south of Sicily. Its location makes it strategically ideal: conquer Malta and its airfields and you can launch strikes anywhere in the Mediterranean. The scars from the many bombardments were still evident while I was there, and that was nine years after the war. The siege of Malta lasted approximately from June 1940 to November 1942. The island and its people were awarded the George Cross for heroism by King George VI in April 1942. By 1944, with the Germans in retreat, life on Malta started to return to some form of normalcy. Still, there was always that thought that the invaders might return.

In January 1945 a major event took place in Malta. It was the arrival of three very important people. The Malta Conference lasted from January 30, 1945, to February 3, 1945. The three VIPs were President Franklin D Roosevelt, British Prime Minister Winston Churchill, and Soviet Premier Joseph Stalin, with their chiefs of staff, who were planning the final campaign of the war. While they were there, the skies above Malta were filled with constant air cover. It remained that way until the VIPs left.

Our navy bases, like most military bases, hire civilians. I found the Maltese I worked with were hard-working and friendly. I was fortunate to be able to get to know several of them. They related some of their experiences to me from the time the German Air Force bombed them around the clock. When the air-raid sirens sounded, they would seek shelter in many of Malta's caves that dotted the island. They remained there until the all-clear was sounded, emerging to realize the destruction that had taken place. Many lost their lives trying to rescue those who were trapped inside bombed-out buildings. Many civilians were crushed to death when buildings collapsed without warning.

Our living quarters were called Nissen Huts. They were made of sheet metal bent into a half-cylinder cemented into the ground, then covered with corrugated steel. The huts were approximately 20 feet long by 10 feet wide and housed eight of us. When it was really hot, the interior felt like the inside of an oven. Doors on each end of the huts were kept open to allow for whatever breeze came by and would circulate inside. At the back end of the hut, near the top, was a fifteen-inch fan that helped draw out the hot air. One day a bird about the size of a sparrow flew in through the open front door. The back door happened to be closed. The bird panicked and began to fly wildly trying to get out, banging into the sides of the hut. Instead of going out the open front door, it flew toward the back of the hut. Our fan was on high, spinning at top speed, propellors a blur. The bird, in its desperate attempt to escape, flew right toward the fan. I watched in horror. Suddenly, it folded its wings and shot through the blades without getting so much as a scratch. We all stood there dumbfounded. No blood, no guts, no feathers, inside or outside of the hut. Truly amazing. I guess birds may have guardian angels too.

About a week after our arrival in Malta, it was time to see the sights. My mentor, Ray Beyers, was willing to show me around. By this time, Beyers considered himself to be a short-timer, so military nomenclature was going by the wayside. To him, the deck was now the floor, bulkheads the wall, the head, the bathroom.

Our trip to Valletta, the capital of Malta, was by bus and it included a detailed travel log, him naming the sights. Ray had been deployed to Malta a couple of times before. Once in the city, we took a walking tour, which led us to Grand Harbour, Malta's bustling seaport. While there, I learned about the oil tanker, SS Ohio, American built but commanded by the British during World War II. The Ohio, along with other oil tankers, were under constant attack by the German air and submarine forces as they fought their way across the Mediterranean Sea to reach port. Repeatedly bombed, strafed, torpedoed, with planes crashing on her deck, she was nearly sunk. The Ohio was the only ship to make Grand Harbour with its cargo of oil and aviation gasoline for the Royal Air Force. Kept afloat with the help of two destroyers, the HMS Penn and HMS Ledbury. Each attached themselves to a side of the ship, keeping it from sinking. Once docked, they off-loaded its precious cargo, then let her sink. Then-Governor, Lord Gort, said, "Had it not been for the Ohio, the island would have been two weeks from surrender."

Valetta, like cities throughout the world, I soon found out, had its seedy side. From the Harbour, we made our way through narrow streets and back alleys, eventually ending up, as Beyers proudly proclaimed, "Welcome to The Gut!"

The Gut was a long narrow street lined with restaurants and bars, mostly bars. As Beyers led the way, I looked up to the second floor of some of the buildings. Women were hanging out the window, arms waving, calling down to us. "I'm Cherry. I'm Cherry." Even though I turned eighteen several months before, and was still somewhat naïve of life in the raw, other than that night at the carnival, I think I knew what that meant.

Halfway down the block, Beyers turned into a bar that had British Navy personnel sitting in one section and some of our guys from the squadron in another. Both groups enjoyed the company of the local ladies as they drank beer.

Beyers took me over to the owner of the bar, a woman he knew who appeared to be in her mid-forties, and introduced me. As I reached out to shake her hand, she pulled down the top of her low-cut blouse exposing her breasts, grabbed my extended hand, and placed it on them, saying, "What do you think?"

Shocked, I jumped backward, banging into a chair where some young gal was sitting, knocked it over, and we both fell on the floor, her dress flying up over her chest. I ended up face-first between her legs, and she wasn't wearing any undergarments. The whole place exploded into laughter, then applause when I helped the young lady up. Totally embarrassed, I ordered a beer, downed it as quickly as I could, and left the bar to return to the base. "Welcome to the Gut!" Ray yelled as I headed out the door.

Our base at Hal Far Airfield was controlled by the Royal Air Force. Their fighter squadrons were at one location on the airfield, and ours at another. They had their missions to accomplish, and we had ours.

A month after I arrived, my supply officer asked me if I wanted to go on one of his missions. It was to be a coordinated exercise with several destroyers and submarines that were part of the Sixth Fleet. I jumped at the chance.

After take-off, we climbed to fifteen hundred feet over the water. The electronic technicians in the back of the P2 were at their screens looking for ships and subs, even though our rendezvous was some time away. I was sitting on a jump seat in the cockpit, staring out the window, and again, fat, dumb, but happy. The PC asked me if I would like to sit in the nose dome and take pictures of the ships when we fly over them. Guess my reply.

I lowered myself down the small crawl space, and with the camera in hand, squeezed past the nose wheel, eased into the canvas-covered seat, and scanned miles and miles of empty ocean ahead of us looking for ships. Before long, there on the horizon, a gray speck. It continued to grow into the shape of a United States Navy Destroyer. It was marvelous and my enthusiasm grew. The PC started to descend to where it seemed as if we were skimming the wave tops, but it was more like 500 to 700 feet above them. Then he made a slight left bank until the ship was broadside to us. I was clicking the camera as fast as I could. When we flew over, I looked down. The sailors on deck were waving at us. Exciting? Yes!

After that, we were on the prowl for subs. The mission lasted about five hours. Back at the base, the photos I took were being developed, and I hoped I didn't screw up. When they came back...Wow! I couldn't believe how well they turned out. Clear, sharply focused, you could see every detail of the ship and its crew. Wow! My dream was coming true.

20

ACOG and RAF

During those many months we were in Malta, our squadron flew hundreds of hours, resulting in a lot of worn-out aircraft parts. Some parts needing replacement were critical enough that the aircraft would be grounded until the part was supplied. These planes were called "ACOG," short for "Aircraft on Ground." Usually, a plane was down for an engine or aircraft inspection, an overhaul, or just waiting for a part to arrive from the States. But there was one time when one of our aircraft was labeled "ACOG," not because of any maintenance problem, but a personnel hygiene issue.

There was always guard duty to do. Day or night. For security reasons the aircraft that weren't flying were buttoned-up, locked down, and access doors closed. One of our airmen recently joined the squadron. Unfortunately, he pulled guard duty while having a bad case of diarrhea. He knew he could not leave his post and there was a crew toilet on board a plane he was guarding. He opened one of the access doors, climbed inside, found the john, and did his business. Then he left, closing the access door, and continued his watch. Of course, with the Mediterranean sun beating down on a closed-up aircraft, the inside temperature can exceed 120 degrees or more.

The following day, a crew member about to do a pre-flight check opened the access door and scrambled inside. He took one whiff and promptly vomited. The rest of the crew refused to fly the aircraft until the odor was eliminated, which took about a day and a half with all access doors and windows opened.

The guard got off with a warning after he stated he couldn't find the flush handle. Being new, he did not know there is no flush handle on this model plane, just a pot you put a paper bag in to catch your waste. But he had to clean up his mess, with all but one window closed. You can bet he learned his lesson.

Sometimes what appears a routine mission can be deadly. A Navy pilot from one of our aircraft carriers that cruised the "Med" had flown in and was to spend the night at the base and leave the following morning to fly back to his ship. I had talked to him when he first arrived since he had to come into our supply office and sign the necessary papers for fuel, and lodging.

That morning, still in our Nissen Huts, we were awakened by the loud, terrible sound, of an aircraft in a power dive, followed by a tremendous crash. A few moments later, the sound of wailing sirens could be heard coming from the base.

When something like that happens, it's "grab your clothes, and get to the base." When I arrived, I learned it was the pilot from the aircraft carrier I had spoken to the day before who crashed and was killed.

Usually, when an accident like that occurs, an explosion and fire follow. But in this instance, none of that happened. Those who witnessed the accident said he appeared to lose control of the A5D on take-off, nosed straight up, spun left, and crashed nose-first into the ground.

The first responders to reach the crash scene initially thought he had been decapitated because his head was missing. They began a search of the area. They found his flight helmet, but no head. Meanwhile, his remains were taken to the infirmary, and while examining the body, the coroner discovered the force of the impact drove his head into his stomach. It was another reminder that flying can be risky.

Anytime I could catch a ride with one of our flight crews, I would jump at the chance. Two of the people I hung around with were from New Jersey. Bill Colville and Armand DeLuca were technicians and part of the flight crews. This particular time, Colville asked if I wanted to go to Tripoli. Of course I did. It just so happened that one of the guys I grew up with was in the Air Force and based there.

The flight to Tripoli was routine. Coming back was another story. About the time we hit the "point-of-no-return," meaning it would take the same amount of flight time to continue to Malta or return to Tripoli, trouble came.

The left engine began running rough and the PC feathered the propeller and shut down the engine. Nothing like seeing a feathered propeller in flight that tells you that your two-engine aircraft just lost 50 percent of its performance.

To offset the loss of the engine, you increase power on the other engine to maintain airspeed and altitude. Except, in this case, the right engine began to overheat. Now it was a question if we were going to be able to make Malta or make it back to Tripoli. The PC elected to continue to Malta but ordered us to put on our parachutes and stand by for two possibilities, just in case the other engine quit: bailout or ditch into the Mediterranean Sea.

Fortunately, we didn't have to do either. We limped back to Malta on one engine. My Guardian Angel was on the job.

Six weeks before we were to return to Brunswick, Maine, an unannounced R5D arrived, taxied to the ramp, parked, and killed its engines. When the cabin door burst open, Top Brass were standing in its doorway. It was a surprise inspection.

The Pentagon wanted to know why a Lieutenant from the RAF was signing our requisitions to purchase supplies for their units. I got called into the office. The inspectors showed me one of the many requisitions I had typed. I looked at Lt. J.B. Klockenkemper, and the officers who were heading up the surprise inspection and burst out laughing. Not a good idea to laugh at your superiors when they are in a foul mood. What was so funny? I explained to them that RAF was my initials, and stood for my name, Robert Allen Frister. I informed them I was trained to always put my initials next to the supply officer's name and rank. It was required to do this initialing no matter who types a requisition. In this case, the requisitions had to always be signed as, Lt. J. B. Klockenkemper, USN/RAF. The surprise inspection came to a screeching halt. They packed up and went back to Washington. Within a month after that episode, out came new stub requisitions that provided a space for the typist's initials. I guess even the Navy can learn a lesson.

21

THE CLUB

My first six months of deployment went rather quickly. Upon our return to Brunswick, our squadron received twelve new airplanes. The P2V-5s were phased out and the new P2V-7s took their place.

The P7s were similar to the P5s. Updated electronic gear for hunting surface vessels and subs was added. The biggest change was the addition of two Westinghouse J-34 jet engines. Each had approximately 3,000 pounds of thrust which increased the P2's airspeed performance. The P2V-5 could cruise at an airspeed of approximately 340 mph; the P2V-7 at 400 mph.

We were scheduled to remain in Brunswick for six months and then return to Malta for another six months. Once back in Brunswick, good things begin to happen. A group of us in our squadron formed a flying club. For 50 dollars you could join, get flying lessons from qualified instructors, or so I thought, gain experience, and add those lessons to your total flying hours.

The club's airplane was a vintage 1940s, tandem-sitting Luscombe that was used as an observation airplane during WWII. It must have seen its share of action. The heater didn't work, so you froze. The noise from the engine was so loud that there were times when you couldn't hear what the instructor was saying. If it was a bumpy ride, you could see an opening of about an inch where the wings and fuselage joined.

We flew our plane out of a small grass-strip airfield near Topsham, Maine.

The approaches to the field had high-voltage power lines on one end and tall trees on the other. There was an open field just beyond the power lines and a split-rail fence defined the airport boundary from the neighboring farmer's field.

Because of those obstructions, we would fly that thing from Topsham to the Lewiston-Auburn Airport, to practice take-offs and landings. All-in-all, it was great. I was getting experience and flying time. However, I did not have my flight logbook with me. I had left it at home in New Jersey not knowing there would be flying clubs available at some Naval Bases. I was told I could log the flying time and get my instructor to sign my form at a later date.

At Topsham, you had to be alert on both your take-offs and landings because of the short and narrow runway, its approaches, and obstructions. On one of our approaches, my instructor took control of the airplane to show me the proper way to perform short-field landings. I, the student, sat in the front seat, with him directly behind me. Thinking he was also going to make the landing, I took my hands off the control stick and throttle. After crossing over the powerlines he began the descent over the open field.

At first, I thought he was showing me how to do a drag-it-in approach, except we were getting lower and lower. I was expecting him to apply power and get the airplane to soar a little higher. He didn't.

Suddenly there was a burst of full power.

Too late! We hit the ground hard and well short of the runway. The plane bounced over the split-rail fence, bounced on the runway, and staggered back into the air. He somehow managed to circle back for a safe landing, the aircraft vibrating badly all around us.

After we landed, some of the flying club guys who were also learning to fly came rushing over. My instructor asked me why I let the airplane get so low.

I replied, "I thought you had the controls to show me the landing."

He said. "No, I thought you had the controls. I only took over when I saw we were going to hit the fence."

The guys who witnessed what happened were more shaken than we were. Then they got pissed. They found out the aircraft had to be grounded for weeks because of the damage. The impact of the hard landing in the field caused the aft portion of the fuselage to be bent at a fifteen-degree angle, which caused the heavy vibration. We were fortunate to get the aircraft back on the ground without losing control. A serious lesson learned: make sure you know who is flying the airplane.

Shortly after that incident, I found out my instructor didn't have a flight instructor rating. He was getting teaching experience to get his rating (certificate). This "detail" kept me from logging any of the flight time we did in the club. Another novice aviator lesson learned: Check credentials.

It took about three weeks before the club got the aircraft back in the air. Unfortunately, it would be its last time.

One of the chiefs who belonged to the flying club was making his solo approach over the power lines and got too low. The landing gear snagged one of the lines which pitched the aircraft in a nose-down attitude. The plane hit the ground and cart-wheeled into a tangled mess. The chief managed to extract himself from the cockpit and walked away with just a few scratches, just before our plane erupted into a ball of fire. Lucky chief. But another setback for my dream of being a flyer.

22

NOT PEACHES AND CREAM

My first year in the Navy went quickly. It seemed every day was an adventure, whether it was getting home to New Jersey—when possible—playing sports, pulling guard duty, or taking part in the everyday activities of a busy squadron, including personnel inspections.

Our squadron's inspections were typically held on our concrete ramp when visiting Top Brass would arrive. There was one good piece of advice I received from one of our chiefs who had been through many VIP inspections before: "Don't lock your knees. Keep a slight bend in them. It will help from tensing up as they pass in front of you." Sure enough, some of the guys were so tense during these inspections that they passed out. There is not much worse than seeing, or hearing, a guy's head bang hard off concrete.

December 31, 1955, New Year's Eve, 11:55 p.m. Three guys had been drinking heavily in the cubicle next to mine. They were making a lot of noise, obviously drunk. Drinking was not allowed in the barracks. But these three always seemed to be making trouble.

I had asked them to take their act down to the lounge and let the rest of us get some sleep. Others were also complaining because they had to get up at 3:30 a.m. for guard duty. An argument ensued. One word leads to another. The guy who I'm jawing with yells, "Come over here and say that." Before I can answer, Parker, one of the guys in my cubicle, yells out, "All my dogs come to me!" The troublemaker comes charging into my cubicle as I jumped down from my bunk. Next thing we're in a fistfight that lasted from 1955 to 1956. Luckily, one of our first-class petty officers who had the watch that evening happened to come onto our floor and broke it up. I ended up with a cut over my left eye where the guy's ring caught me. He ended up with a black eye and a bloody nose. They moved their party to the lounge.

It wasn't long after that incident that tragedy struck.

Two of those troubled guys were partying in Lewiston, not the guy I fought with, and were going from bar to bar, getting drunk. For some unknown reason, they got into an argument with each other. They then went into an alley and got into a fistfight. The next day they found one of the two dead in the alley, his head bashed in. The other guy was arrested for murder. He went to trial and was convicted of manslaughter. But before he was sentenced, a woman came forward stating she had seen the whole thing.

According to her statement, she saw the two men fighting in the alley. The one who was convicted left the alley, but the victim, for some unknown reason, started climbing up the side of a two-story post office building. The building, made of brick, was layered so it had just enough crevices for a hand-and-toe hold to climb up the side. That is what the deceased did. When he reached the top and tried to get onto the roof, she said, he lost his balance, fell, and landed headfirst onto the concrete floor of the alleyway. She said that was why his head was bashed in. Asked why she did not speak up during the trial, she replied, "I didn't want to get involved. But my conscious bothered me so much that I had to come forward." It reminded me of a time I did not speak up.

In the Spring of 1956, our squadron was slated to go back to Malta. Before we did, I caught a P2 fam-flight (familiarization flight) our squadron would often take to Bermuda and then return the same day. Bermuda's airport was used by both civilians and military, ours being out in left field. While the crew was in flight operations, preparing for our return, I decided to go for a swim off one of the Bermuda jetties near the runway.

I stripped to my shorts and dove in. The water was clear and refreshing. I swam about 50 yards from the jetty and the next thing I noticed, swimming near me, was a Barracuda. More were showing up. Have you ever seen a

Barracuda up close, almost eye-to-eye? These Barracuda appeared to be about four feet long, silvery, with fang-like teeth and fearsome-looking eyes, that was staring at me as though I might be dinner.

It took me about two seconds to realize what attracted them. The metal dog tags and the St. Christopher Medal I had on were acting like fishing lures, spinning as I swam. I beat a hasty retreat and got out of the water as quickly as I could, hoping none of them were going to grab my medals, or me. That close call made me wonder if some of those stories you hear about shark attacks may be linked to victims wearing those kinds of medals.

Once our squadron was back in Malta, the Egyptian Suez Canal Zone Crisis became the topic of the day. Not far from our Hal Far airbase was Luga Airfield, where the Royal Air Force was using Valiant and Canberra Bombers on night raids to attack the Zone.

At Hal Far, the Royal Navy had squadrons of De Haviland Vampires, Hawker Sea Hawks, the Fairy Ganett, and more. They also had a top aerobatic team called the "Ace of Diamonds" that practiced flying with their Hawker Sea Hawks. Watching their rehearsal was breathtaking. Four aircraft would fly over the airfield from opposite directions and cross over one another at no more than what seemed like a few feet separating them. They would then zoom skyward into a star burst, reverse direction, and land. All work would stop, not because of their aerobatics, but because we all thought we were about to see a mid-air collision. Thank heavens that never happened.

But the British did have several accidents while I was there.

23

MALTA INCIDENTS

One of the accidents occurred when a British plane lost engine power and landed in the Mediterranean Sea. This time, the pilot was rescued. Another accident I witnessed ended tragically.

It happened when the pilot was taking off. My understanding at the time was that while on the ground, the pilot would put the gear handle lever in the up position. As he left the ground, the landing gear would start to retract, which would reduce the drag from the landing gear, helping the plane gain airspeed quicker. In this case, as the pilot roared down the runway, a sudden gust of wind lifted the aircraft off the ground before it attained its flying airspeed. This kept the pilot from climbing and the aircraft was on the verge of stalling. As it continued down the runway, the left-wing tip scraped the runway, then the right tip did as well. The plane rocked back and forth like that until it reached the end of the runway. Malta is known for its short stone-wall fences that appear all over the island. These walls indicate the owner's property line. At the end of the runway was a farmer's field, and a stone wall. The aircraft hit the wall, glanced off the rocks, and went airborne. The plane then banked left, sheared off the side of the farmer's roof, inverted, and crashed in a blazing ball of fire. The pilot did not survive.

During that time, our squadron was establishing a new fleet record for our Neptunes. We had logged over 1,000 flying hours of ASW combat training missions in two consecutive months, earning our squadron the Navy's "E" award for "Excellence." This award is one of the highest distinctions paid to a combat squadron. After the award was granted, a big "E" was proudly sported on each of our Neptunes.

This was also about the time I passed the exams that led to my going up a grade in the Navy. I was now a Third-Class Aviation Storekeeper. My friends and I celebrated by going down to the "gut" for some refreshments.

That night, the bar was crowded with sailors from the British and our navies, enjoying the evening drinking beer and listening to the live entertainment. Even though we were wearing civilian clothes, you could tell who was military and who was not. Haircuts. One of the chiefs from our squadron, who I knew as a quiet, laid-back, gentleman, who usually kept to himself, had a few too many beers before he joined us.

No sooner did the entertainers leave the stage for their break when the chief got up and weaved his way to it. Once there, he grabbed one of the microphones the entertainers used and made the following announcement, "Ladies and gentlemen, may I have your attention?" He was slurring the words.

The bar was full of sailors with their wives and girlfriends. Everyone stopped talking and focused their attention on the chief. I expected something foreboding to be revealed, especially with all that was going on in Egypt.

The chief, assured he had all of our attention, unzipped his trousers, put his hand inside, and began fumbling around.

The women began screaming. Guys knocked over chairs as they raced to the stage.

The chief, unfazed by all the commotion, pulled out a pocket watch attached to a long chain, and announced, "The time is now 8:30." He then stuffed the watch back in his pants, zipped up, and calmly walked off the stage and right out the door.

There was one more incident that happened while in Malta. There was a free-for-all in that same bar.

Sailors, especially those that have been out to sea for months at a time, often received liberty in Malta. As many beers and drinks were downed, bottled-up emotions sometimes exploded into the open. One remark can lead to another, and just like in the movies, the result may be fist-fights, chairs flying, bottles breaking, police arriving, and sailors scattering.

Hal Far Airbase was always a beehive of activity with its two runways, the RAF doing their flying and our squadron doing ours. There was no such thing as a dull moment. At times, it could be downright dangerous.

I happened to be working in our supply storage area, which was close to an active runway with my back to it. Suddenly, a nose wheel from one of our P2s came whizzing past the right side of my head. I turned to see a P2 had landed on its nose wheel and it sheared off, sending it in my direction at more than a hundred miles an hour. The stub of the nose-gear strut was still digging into the pavement and trailing a shower of sparks before it came to a stop. Out came the emergency trucks, followed by our maintenance crew. The runway was shut down while they repaired the damage. Because Hal Far had two runways, that incident didn't disrupt any other take-offs and landings. But it sure disrupted my confidence that I was safe in the supply office.

Malta was a haven for people who liked the water. You had to like water since Malta is an island. You could swim 365 days a year due to its warm weather and warm water. The guys with who I hung around would, on occasion, climb some of the rocky and rugged cliffs that overlooked the Mediterranean, some rising hundreds of feet. Then came, "I dare you." It was like the dares I heard growing up. The dare? Who would dive from the highest perch?

Three of us began our climb. Two stopped at about 30 feet above the water. I went twenty-feet higher. Once we reached our goal, we did a swan dive and hit the water. It was like hitting a brick wall. Dare, or no dare, I decided no more of that.

There was also a cove called "Octopus Creek," where we would swim. The Creek was a narrow inlet where waves from the Mediterranean Sea came crashing in against the rocks. Colville, DeLuca, and I would spend many a day swimming there. My first time, I was standing on a rock ledge, the water up to my chest, just relaxing and feeling the beat of the waves. Then

I felt something like kelp caressing my right leg. Thinking that was what it was, I looked down in the crystal-clear water. To my surprise, I saw a foot-and-a-half octopus beginning to wrap its tentacles around my right leg. I don't know who was more shook-up, me or the octopus, because it turned white. I made a hasty retreat out of the Creek. I knew then why they called it Octopus Creek.

Three months into our deployment, our squadron decided to have a beach party five miles from the base. Instead of joining the rest of the group who were going by bus, Colville and I decided to swim to the beach.

Colville and I always prided ourselves on being strong swimmers. It was only about four miles from Octopus Creek to Marsaklokk Bay where the party was being held. The bay was also a very busy harbor with a stream of inbound and outbound ships. Swimming there was not a good idea.

After about two miles and as we entered the harbor, Colville began getting leg cramps. They became so painful, he had trouble swimming. We trod water for about fifteen minutes to see if the cramps would subside. When they didn't, we decided to turn back. We kept stopping to tread water, long enough to catch a breath, rub his cramps, swim another hundred yards, and repeat the same sequence. Two hours later, exhausted, we dragged ourselves upon the rocky shore, happy to be back on dry land.

The following day, a British sailor, who had been swimming in the same area where our beach picnic was held, was killed by a great white shark. That didn't stop us from swimming, but we kept a wary eye out for these predators.

24

BLIMPS

I wasn't the only one who had advanced in rate. One was a first-class aviation mechanic who was promoted to chief aviation mechanic. His promotion almost proved deadly.

Normally, our squadron's aircraft were parked on the main (apron) ramp. Others were parked farther away and were usually going through periodic maintenance checks. As I walked across the back apron toward our barracks, I notice three of our mechanics standing next to one of our P2's four-bladed propellers. As a prank, two of the mechanics tied the new chief to the prop and were taking his picture. I happened to glance up at the cockpit and saw another mechanic sitting in the PC seat. He moved forward as if reaching for something. It must have been the engine start switch because the prop blade moved about six inches. The chief started screaming to cut him loose. I was waiting for the engine to roar to life and chop him up. Thank God it didn't. The other mechanics quickly untied him. When they did, his knees buckled, and he fell to the ground. He lay there for several minutes before he could stand. I believed he fainted. What was meant to be a prank could have ended up tragically. Had any of our officers seen it, all four of them would be reduced to a grade lower than mine. Some joke. Another lesson learned.

Near the end of September 1956, my time with the squadron came to an end. As in all military branches, you're in a unit for only so long, then you get transferred. I had been with VP-11 for almost two years, a wonderful two years, and enjoyed the company of many friends.

I said goodbye to my Maltese friends, my squadron mates, and the "Gut." I hopped aboard an R5D that took off in a heavy rainstorm as we left for NAS (Naval Air Station) Port Lyautey, French Morocco. I would only spend one night there but did get a chance to see how the real belly dancers perform at a local Brasserie (bar). Very interesting.

The next day I was on my way back to the States. Ahead lay NAS Glynco, Brunswick, Georgia. But before that, a furlough.

I contacted my friend Gene Horton, and we talked about old times. He asked if I was in touch with Barbara. I said we hadn't seen or talked to one another in almost two years, and she probably had forgotten me. I didn't mention I had awakened one night in Malta, telling myself that I was going to marry Barbara. He urged me to call her.

I reluctantly called, afraid she might hang up.

I was very surprised Barbara accepted my invitation to go out. After that, we started dating regularly. She later told me she had written a letter to me while I was in Malta, but never mailed it. We concluded that it was nearly the same night I woke up thinking I would marry her.

Before long, my furlough was over, and it was, "Hello Brunswick, Georgia." Barbara and I kept in touch the old-fashioned way, through the United States Post Office. No emails, no cellphones, no texting back and forth then.

NAS Glynco (Glynn County) was like going from the modern Navy, to somewhere back in time. Instead of P2s, Brunswick was the base of two ZP (ZP means lighter than air) squadrons of Navy blimps, jet-fighters, and Lockheed's Super Constellations (EC-121's), Warning Star. The blimps were my main focus.

My new assignment was not with a flying squadron, but a FASRON (Fleet Aviation Supply Squadron.) Our job was to supply all of the base squadrons with parts. I would have preferred being in one of the ZP's squadrons, a flying squadron, but you go where the navy sends you.

In the 1920s, 1930s, and 1940s, the Navy had many airships, classified as ZPs. The most famous of these were the USS Akron, USS Macon, USS Los

Angeles, and the USS Shenandoah. They were classified as "a-rigid," because of their internal steel construction and Ballonets (gas bags) that held the Helium. Blimps, on the other hand, had only the Ballonets and therefore were affectionately called "poopy bags." They were classified as "b-limp." Thus "blimps."

As graceful as those "lighter-than-air" airships looked, they could become dangerous, especially in stormy weather. Many were lost during those early years due to thunderstorms, lightning strikes, training accidents, or botched take-offs and landings. Three of the four most famous airships, The USS Akron, The USS Macon, and The USS Shenandoah, broke up in flight due to adverse weather, with the loss of many Navy personnel. The last of the four, the Los Angeles, had a brilliant career before it was decommissioned in 1932.

Throughout World War II, blimps were used for our coastal protection, hunting enemy ships and submarines. They also escorted convoys. At that time, they were the pride of the aviation fleet for coastal duty.

They were slow, graceful looking, and looked like a dark storm cloud coming your way. One of their main advantages was they could cruise at a lower airspeed than a conventional aircraft and stay aloft for more than twenty hours. That meant enemy submarines had to remain underwater longer than they wanted and could be easily spotted as the blimps slowly flew overhead.

Built by Goodyear, the blimps had two 600 HP Pratt & Whitney Engines and cruised at 60 miles per hour. The airships had a length of 310 feet, held 625,000 cubic feet of Helium, and could carry a payload of 10,000 pounds. A center landing wheel under the Gondola was used for take-offs and landings.

To house these giants, the hangars were enormous. Glynco had two wooden hangars, each over 1,000 feet long, 300 feet wide, and 200 feet tall. Each blimp squadron, ZP-2, and ZP-3 had approximately eight blimps. When not airborne, they were either tethered to a 20-ton metal mooring mast, or inside the hangar. A "pressure watch" sailor was assigned to monitor the pressure in the bags from inside the gondola. With too much pressure, the blimp rose; too little, it began to droop and if not checked, could deflate.

Re-positioning blimps in and out of the hangar could be dangerous, especially on a windy day. Doing maintenance while a blimp was inside the hangar was also risky. Part of the maintenance checks required inspecting the top of the airship for rips and tears, and patching any found. In one case, a hangar door was being opened when a gust of wind lifted the blimp, its top hitting the hangar ceiling. A sailor who was on top of the blimp performing repairs was nearly crushed to death when it pinned him against one of the rafters.

The launching and the landing of a blimp also had their dangers. The blimp would roll about 100 feet on its one wheel, lift off, point its nose skyward, two handling lines dangling from its bow, and be gracefully on its way. Usually, its destination was the Atlantic Ocean, assigned to whatever mission it was to accomplish that day.

Landing, however, was something else, especially if it was windy. In would come this three-hundred-foot "gray cloud," its nose pointed down, engines roaring, handling lines dangling, while fifty ground handlers—I was one of them on several occasions—would rush out to secure it. Twenty-five men would grab one line, and the other twenty-five grabbed the other, narrowly avoiding the eighteen-inch propellers that could slice a man into pieces. Once the line was safely held, we had to run like hell toward the mooring mast. The man on top of the mast waited as the pilot maneuvered the blimp into position, then with a final burst of its engines, made contact with the mast. A clip would be latched and the blimp would finally be secured. Everybody sighed in relief. Until the next blimp approached.

Another cardinal rule of securing Blimps: let go of the lines if the Blimp starts to rise without warning or you might go up with it. There had been incidents where that happened. One was captured on film in 1932. The USS Akron aborted its landing and three of the mooring crew failed to let go of the rope. They were hauled hundreds of feet into the air. Two fell to their deaths. The third managed to hold on until the Akron landed safely. Blimps were like sharks, beautiful to watch but dangerous if you made the wrong move. I learned to respect the men who handled these magnificent flying machines but still itched to be an airplane pilot. Was I getting any closer?

25

THE TOM COLLINS CAPER

I spent one year at NAS Glynco and learned a little bit about Brunswick's history. Like the rest of America's towns and cities, Brunswick had its history with Native American Indians. They were called the Mocamas but were eventually wiped out by diseases. While I was there, you couldn't go anywhere without hearing or seeing the name of a man called Oglethorpe.

In the middle 1700s, James Oglethorpe built the town of Frederica on St. Simons Island in defiance of the Spaniards who had laid claim to the island. Eventually, the Spanish were driven off by the British, and Oglethorpe was the local hero and honored ever since. The famed Hotel Oglethorpe, named after him, was very popular while I was there.

Brunswick was another ship-building seaport city. During WWII, it was the home of the J. A. Jones Construction Company, known for their Liberty Class Ships that transported our troops to battle zones. They produced an average of one ship every 90 days. They sent 99 of their vessels into the war effort. Brunswick was also known for its thriving shrimp industry.

For a very short time, I managed to continue taking flying lessons from a flight school called Tidewater Aviation, at a local airport. The flight school used a Piper Pa-17, called a Vagabond N4666H, for training. That turned into a flying nightmare. My instructor wasn't the best. I think he was still fighting the civil war, especially knowing I was navy and from the north. His manner was harsh when it came to instruction, and I was getting pretty fed up with it. The crowning blow occurred as we started practicing approaches to landing by aiming at one of the crowded beaches that stretched along St. Simons Island.

We would begin our final approach as though we were landing at the airport, then watch the people on the beach scatter in alarm when we almost touched down. He would start laughing, pull up, and then do it again. When we got back to the airport, I told him that was it. One hour and thirty minutes of his stupidity were enough. Why he was never reported to the CAB is still a mystery to me. I decided the rest of my flying lessons would be after I was discharged and when they could be paid for through the Korean G.I Bill.

Part of FASRON's responsibility was fueling the aircraft. They used mostly civilian employees to do that as well as other jobs. When any of the tanker trucks ran out of fuel it would be up to its driver to go to the fuel dump and replenish their supply. For safety reasons, all aviation gas was stored in underground bunkers covered by mounds of dirt and grass in case of a fire. The greatest concern was lightning strikes which could ignite the fuel.

To refuel and operate the control valves, a man had to go down into a narrow eight-foot-deep pit. It was much like going down a street man-hole. Inside the pit, the air was always heavy with the smell of gas fumes.

One day, a driver went to the bunker but did not return, which was unusual. I was asked to go to see what was keeping him, but I was busy with another job. Another sailor took my place. When he arrived, he found the driver lying at the bottom of the pit, dead.

During the accident investigation, they noted the victim had a large bump on his head. We were not sure if he slipped going down the metal ladder and knocked himself out or if he was overcome by the fumes while in the pit, fainted, and struck his head when he fell. After that, two people were required to do the refueling to prevent any more accidents.

Navy work took a lot of time, but there was also time for recreation. I enjoyed playing sports for the Navy. I played softball and basketball against local teams. Sometimes we would travel the short distance to Florida and play other naval bases.

One hot and muggy night, the group I played with decided to go to one of the local bars for a few beers after a basketball game. We hadn't eaten and were pretty dehydrated. While there, one of the sailors I hung around with, asked me if I ever had a Tom Collins drink. I said no. He said to try one. I did. I told him I'd rather drink a beer. "Try another one," he urged. "Okay," I said.

After a while, we decided to go to dinner, each in our car. I remember walking to my car, opening the door, and getting in. Then things began to get a little fuzzy once I got behind the wheel. I woke up the next morning in jail. And I wasn't alone. Three other sailors were in the cell with me—not the ones with me at the bar—each of these guys was charged with fighting, drinking, and creating a public disturbance. Incredibly, they were all released.

But I was still being held. Someone posted a bail bond for me. The guy who convinced me to try a Tom Collins found a bondsman to get me released. However, before that happened, I was considered absent without leave (AWOL) for not being at muster that morning. Deep trouble. Maybe a Captain's Mast.

That morning, I was still pretty well hungover. By the time I woke up, the other sailors had been released. Shortly after that, the guard brought me breakfast. He slid a tin plate under the cell door with hominy grits covered in pork gravy. I took one look and nearly vomited. Then I remembered seeing an old gangster movie where the prisoner kicked the same kind of breakfast back under the bottom of the cell door. I gave it a quick kick. The plate slid under the door, slammed up against the wall, and flipped over, splattering the wall and floor with grits and gravy. What they didn't show in the movie was that you had to clean up that mess.

Things were going from bad to worst. If you have never found yourself in a jail cell, let me clue you in. Four bunk beds, one washbasin, one toilet, one mirror made of polished metal, and hours of wondering how the hell you got yourself into this jam.

Of course, there comes that time when you have to relieve yourself. While doing so, I heard a female voice say, "You really look good this morning."

Surprised? Yes! I almost lost a part of my lower anatomy zipping up.

After several minutes of conversation, and even though I couldn't see her,

I found out why she was in jail. She had been arrested for loitering and was serving a 90-day sentence, of which, she had served 45 days. She then wanted to know if I would pick her up after she was released. I said no. That brought our conversation to an abrupt end.

After my release, I found out my friendly female cellmate was a prostitute. One of the guys I knew who was arrested for a DUI several weeks later was put into the same cell where I had been and told me about her. He also was surprised hearing a woman's voice as he was relieving himself. In his case, he struck up a conversation with her and began dating her after her release. Several months later they were married. A group of us tried to talk him out of it, but he wouldn't listen. I can only imagine what they might have said when someone who didn't know the circumstances asked them how they met.

The one question that always baffled me was how she could see me, or any other guy, relieving ourselves in that cell without us being able to see her. Before they were married, her husband-to-be told me it was relatively easy on her part. The cells had been designed with aisles on both sides and both the men's and woman's cells were on the same row. She would take out her pocket mirror and hold it out of the cell far enough to be able to see the cell mirror which was angled down toward the toilet bowl. She could see us, but we couldn't see her. Hmmm. What thoughts were going through her mind?

During the time I was in that cell, I tried to recall the events that took place the preceding night, but it was pretty much a blur.

Once I was released, those with me that night said that I got into my car and began driving. I drove through a stop sign and just missed hitting a parked police car. I then drove down Brunswick's main street with the police car following, its red lights flashing. Finally, I turned into a Greyhound Bus Station's parking lot and stopped. From there it was off to the police station in custody.

On top of all the trouble I was already in, I had to worry about being court marshaled for being AWOL.

Lucky for me, my division officer told me not to worry, since I had never been in any trouble before. He also said it would not be part of my record. I was grateful for that.

I still had to appear before a judge who would sentence me for getting ticketed. I was worried I would lose my driver's license, not only in Georgia but also in New Jersey. Thankfully, that didn't happen. The judge fined me $164 for a DUI and court costs, which was about the same amount the Navy paid me monthly. That was a lot of money in those days, so he gave me several weeks to pay it.

Someone suggested I call home and ask my parents for the money. Some of the guys even offered me a few dollars to help pay for my fines. I told them I appreciated their offer but no thank you. I was not about to trouble my parents or take money from my friends. I managed to get myself into this mess and I would get myself out of it. How?

26

TURNING POINT

I had made up my mind that since I created my mess, I had to figure out how to clean it up without the help of my parents and friends. Hello, integrity. Hello, Seabrook Seafood Company.

The Seabrook company owned a shrimp factory in Brunswick which was located next to a pier where the shrimp boats docked. And where I would have a very short career off-loading shrimp boats for the next several weekends.

After the boat's dock, our job would be to offload shrimp and transfer them to the processing area in the plant. Then the shrimp would be separated by the different sizes, cleaned, packaged, and sent nationwide. Like any fish market, there was a heavy odor of dead seafood. It hangs in the air and clings to your clothes. It's the kind of smell that attracts stray cats, meowing loudly near the entrance of the factory looking for a handout. As if that wasn't bad enough, the strays would follow me as I walked down the street to my car. (But I don't think this odor was as bad as being downwind of a Georgia pulp mill when they were operating.) Once back at the barracks, guys would look at me, pinch their noses and point urgently to the shower.

It took me a long time before I could eat shrimp again. Especially after seeing how they were prepared from trawler to factory to shipping. Eventually, what little money I had saved, and what I was earning from this job, allowed me to pay the fine. All looked well.

When my day in court came, I made the mistake of asking the judge who fined me where the $164 was going. Wrong thing to ask.

The judge said I had ten seconds to get out of his court before he would fine me for contempt and give me a few more nights in jail. I beat a hasty retreat and haven't had a Tom Collins since.

The year I spent in Brunswick was enjoyable, other than spending that night as a guest of the town. Our FASRON employed many civilians, and quite a few—mostly women—worked with me as clerical secretaries. Other civilian employees, all male, worked in our supply warehouses.

While stationed there, I took the required exams for an upgrade in rate. I passed them and became a second-class petty officer. More Pay. More responsibility.

While I was at the base, I found the civilians who worked in our supply department were very friendly. There was not the, "you're Navy and I'm a civilian" type of atmosphere that may be prevalent at some military bases. On many occasions, I would be invited to attend their picnics, beach parties, or other occasions.

My time with Uncle Sam was getting short. My 21st birthday was only several months away when President Eisenhower, who had been cutting back on the military, allowed early discharges. That meant I would be getting out of the Navy three months before my 21st birthday. Hooray!

On October 4, 1957, I received my honorable discharge papers. I said goodbye to the people who I had been working with and to my shipmates. (One of whom I would meet unexpectedly eight years later. A meeting I won't forget.)

I jumped into my 1955 Pontiac Chieftain and pointed its nose toward the main gate with the thought that I was soon to be free from all the regimentation of the past three years. I was looking forward to a new career.

So, there I was driving along, fat, dumb, and happy, listening to the music on the radio. Suddenly the music stopped. An announcer came on and said, "We interrupt this program with a special news bulletin. The Russians have just launched Sputnik, the first satellite ever to be launched into space. Stand by for more news as we receive it. Now back to our regularly scheduled program."

Panic set in. The news of the Soviet launch stunned the world. For me, all I could imagine was that the gate in front of me that was now open was going to be closed before I got there. The guards weren't going to let anyone off the base. Not even those who had just been discharged, namely me.

I stepped on the Duck's gas pedal. (The Duck was the name I gave to my car. I gave names to all the cars I owned. Remember my 36 Dodge "Big Al," named after a movie I had seen about gangster Al Capone. The idea came from my dad who had given names to his cars, our sleds, or, just about anything that you could ride. The 55 Pontiac I now owned was named after Disney's cartoon character, "Donald Duck." Barbara and I had won a small Donald Duck porcelain figure on the Asbury Park pier, and I had attached it to my car's glare shield.) I was really afraid the guards would keep the Duck from passing through the gate to freedom.

The gate stayed open. I showed my discharge papers to the guards, and they waved me through. I took one last look at NAS Glynco through my rearview mirror and said goodbye to the United States Navy.

I was now a civilian and homeward-bound. I was older and I believed somewhat wiser in the ways of the world, but still had that starry-eyed dream of becoming an airline pilot. As I gazed up at the sky, wanting to touch the stars, I wondered what lay ahead.

27

RETURN

Now came the time to separate the apples from the oranges. First came the process of having the government approve my application for the Korean GI Bill. It would become a longer process than I anticipated.

In the interim, I took the exam to become a mailman for the Dover Post Office, passed it, and was hired shortly thereafter. Initially, I was hired as a substitute mail carrier, filling in for the mailmen who were out sick or on vacation. One of the routes I was given coincidentally was the street where Barbara lived and where I would take my lunch break. How nice.

Delivering mail was a unique experience. The mailman's creed is well known, "Neither snow, wind, or rain shall deter these men from making their appointed rounds." What they left out was protecting yourself from stray animals that found your legs appetizing. Or, from some irate person whose mail arrived too late in the day. Or delivering packages or mail marked, "Special Delivery."

Special Deliveries were top-priority mail and were usually delivered early in the morning. Once at the house, you hoped the people were up, ring the doorbell, and wait. Most of the time the recipients were home and signed for their mail. If they weren't available, you would bring the SD back to the post office.

On a couple of those early morning occasions when I rang the doorbell, it would open and there would be this woman standing in her see-through negligee, no robe, still half-asleep, sign for the mail, say thank you, and close the door. How trusting. And, how nice.

You know that famous thing dog owners say: "My dog doesn't bite." They should add, "me." But if you're a mailperson, be on guard. Some of the mailmen I worked with had been with the post office for many years, so they carried a water pistol filled with a mixture of ammonia and water. A couple of quick sprays on a dog's nose sent them scurrying in another direction. It may sound cruel, but I witnessed what a dog bite can do to someone's leg.

There is one incident that stands out from that time. It snowed rather heavily for several days and mail delivery had been stopped until the streets and sidewalks were cleared. That meant no delivery for anyone for the next three days. Once we began operating again, I came to a home where the sidewalk hadn't been cleared. Although we were told we did not have to deliver the mail in this kind of case, I waded through the snow anyway up the sidewalk to the porch. Just as I was putting the mail into the mailbox, the front door flew open and this old guy came out of his house and grabbed me by the throat screaming, "Where have you been?" After I pried his hands from around my neck, I managed to calm him down, really not knowing what set him off.

It was the beginning of the month when Social Security checks were sent to retirees. This guy had to be in his eighties and he wasn't going anywhere, not with the driveway and sidewalk covered with snow. It was just that he had to have that social security check in hand. I didn't realize until then how our senior citizens relied on our government's social security checks and their pensions. Now I do.

In January 1958, I finally received approval for my GI Bill. Because I elected not to go to a four-year college, but to apply to an aviation school to get my pilot's licenses, the government would pay me a total of $1,247.68. I also had $300 I received as a mustering-out payment. (The $1,247.68 was calculated on my being in service from September 9, 1954, to October 4, 1957, 3 years and 19 days @ $1.12 per day for each day I was in the navy. That equates to 1,114 days of military duty.)

Now that I knew just how much I was to receive from my GI Bill, it was time to contact flight schools. I was surprised there were many.

After careful research, there was only one flight school I thought would be the best, Parks Air College in East St. Louis, Illinois. My research indicated Parks was the only one with an extraordinary history of training pilots.

Oliver Parks founded the school in 1927, not long after Lindbergh's historic flight from New York to Paris. During World War II, the school and its subsidiaries trained approximately one of every ten Army Air Corps pilots, plus thousands of aircraft mechanics. The school also offered courses in Aviation Sciences, Engineering, and Physics and was a part of St. Louis University.

But there was another reason I eliminated New Jersey flight schools. Barbara and I were always open to traveling with a "what's over the horizon" attitude. As Horace Greely once said, "Go West young man." Now that we had set our sights on what flight school I wanted to attend, Barbara and I set the date March 30, 1958 to get married.

After our reception at my folk's house, like the pioneers who traveled westward in their Conestoga wagons, iron horses (trains), we jumped into our "iron pony" automobile, pointed its nose west, and left for Parks Air College the same day.

28

NEWLYWEDS & FLYING SCHOOL

Newlyweds with no jobs, we had a few hundred dollars that Barbara saved, and gift money from our wedding, so we felt our future looked bright. The $1,247.68 from the Korean G I Bill was set aside for my flight instructions, which wasn't cheap.

Barbara found employment at the Union Bank in East St. Louis, which lies just across the Mississippi River from St Louis.

The one drawback: I couldn't start my flight training until May. Thanks to people at Parks who found a job for me at the Metropolitan Airport working for Walston Aviation, no more than a stone's throw from Parks College's Airport. My title: "line-boy."

My job was to fuel, polish, and clean airplanes, and do all the other odd jobs that come up at an airport. The pay was $1 per hour, forty hours a week, which equated to just enough income to pay for our groceries. Barbara's income from the bank, a tad more than what I was making, helped cover the monies still needed for the flight training, rent, and what little entertainment we could afford. But we persevered.

At the time, I intended to secure a commercial pilot's license, multi-engine rating, instrument rating, and flight instructor rating. It cost $2,500 to obtain a commercial pilot rating. The instrument and instructor ratings were $600 to $700 each, and the multi-engine rating was $450. All these fees were based on me completing each sequence with the minimum number of flight hours required for those licenses. That seldom happens.

Once the $1,247.68 the government allotted me was spent, the rest was out-of-pocket. We couldn't afford it all, so I decided to go for the commercial pilot and multi-engine ratings.

Money was a big problem. Fortunately, we found a small cottage that backed up to Park's airport. All I had to do was hop a fence, cross the main runway, and walk to flight operations for my flying lessons whenever Barbara needed to use our car to go to work. Unfortunately, the cottage had one problem which we didn't know about when we first moved into it.

Rats!

The cottage had a dirt basement that was dark, damp, and musty. We believed that at one time it must have been flooded but had not given it much thought. Several nights after we moved in, as we lay in bed, we heard gnawing sounds coming from our pantry where we stored our dry goods. Rats were eating their way through the drywall to get at the food we stored there. We told our landlady the next day. Her answer: "buy traps," which we did, and also bought a cat. We caught several rodents with the traps. The cat? None. The rat problem ceased about a week after using the traps. We lived in that cottage for a year and a half without another rat incident.

Park's airfield consisted of two cinder-based runways, approximately 100 feet wide and 1600 long. Several hangars housed the aircraft I would be trained on. One was a Cessna 170, a taildragger (that refers to aircraft having a tail-wheel instead of a nose-wheel), and the other was a twin-engine Cessna T-50 Bobcat, also a taildragger, which the Army Air Force called the UC-78.

The first of my lessons began with a grouchy old flight instructor named Charlie Parish. After several hours of flying with him, I began to suspect he was a relative of the Tidewater Aviation instructor I had while at Brunswick. Nothing I did was right. I couldn't get into or out of the airplane right. He would chew me out for one thing or another. It was getting to the point where I thought I was back in the military. This went on from the beginning of May until the end of August. Finally, I had enough and went to the chief pilot and asked for a change of instructors. It was like going from night to day.

Charles Gaedig was truly a darn-good flight instructor and I enjoyed being taught by him. He was one of the pilots who flew C-46 Commandos over the Hump during WWII. I was grateful he would be my instructor for the next year and a half, helping me to obtain my commercial pilot and multi-engine certificates.

The difference between flying a taildragger as opposed to a conventional tri-cycle type aircraft is similar to learning to drive an automobile with an automatic transmission vs a standard shift. The difference is most noticeable when you change gears using the clutch and hear the grinding noise when you mess it up.

Tri-cycle landings are done by landing on the two main landing gears and then lowering the nose wheel. There is much less chance of losing control of the airplane. On the other hand, the taildragger requires you do a three-point landing by touching down with the main wheels and the tail wheel at the same time. You try to avoid the possibility of ground-looping and ending up going backward down the runway.

The C-170 was an all-metal aircraft that had a 100 HP Continental Engine. It could cruise at 140 mph and had a stall speed of approximately 30 mph.

The Cessna Aircraft Company, at that time, had other taildraggers: the C-120, C-140, C-170, C-180, and the C-195. All had what I called, "spring gear." Land a little hard, and that spring gear could sling-shot you back six feet in the air. If you didn't recover by adding a little burst of power and gently landing, you would keep bouncing down the runway with a "let's go around and try that again," on your lips.

It always makes me laugh when I hear someone say, "flying is no different from driving a car." Oh, really? Here's just a quick course on what you are required to learn before obtaining your pilot's license.

Let's start your lesson by just trying to keep your wings level, maintaining your altitude, and learning how to take-off and land, followed by cross-wind T & Ls, power on and power off (throttle at idle), stalls, slips, short field T & Ls, slow flight, steep turns, forced landings. And that's just for starters.

Next up: how to properly distribute the weight and balance of the aircraft you're going to fly. An aircraft isn't a truck or automobile where you keep putting everything including the kitchen sink into them until the springs sag. Overload an airplane and it probably won't get off the ground. Keeping accurate aircraft maintenance records is a must.

Then comes cross-country flying and beginning to understand weather patterns. You need to learn how properly file flight plans. Plotting the course, or courses, you intend to fly means you need to learn how to read a sectional chart, an area map of the course you will be flying, noting the outstanding landmarks along your flight path such as towns, lakes railroads, highways, etcetera, etcetera, etcetera.

My instructor, Charles Gaedig, had a simple verse to help students remember how to plot a course. I never forgot it and used it when I taught my students to plot a course to fly across the country. It goes like this, "True virgins make dull companions." Each word's starting letter has an important meaning:

T= true course from point A to point B.

V=variation, plus or minus to your true course gives you your M=magnetic heading

D=drift. en-route wind aloft direction and velocity, left or right drift, gives you a

C=compass heading

TVMDC= "True virgins make dull companions!"

Part of preparing for any pilot's license or rating is the FAA written and oral exams you must pass. Finally, on November 28, 1958, I passed my FAA (Federal Aviation Administration) check ride and obtained my Private Pilot's License. (It is interesting to note, that had I taken my check-ride a month earlier, it would have been from the CAA (Civil Aeronautics Administration) which later became the FAA.)

With that first obstacle behind me, my flying could become more advanced as I geared toward getting my commercial pilot certificate. I had taken a big step toward achieving my dream but still had a long way to go.

29

DANGER AT THE METRO

Being a line boy at the "Metro" had its moments. There was the day I heard the roar of an aircraft engine as the pilot applied full power for his take-off. I glanced over at the runway and watched as the C-170 lifted off. Ten feet into the air, it suddenly pitched straight up, banked a sharp left, and fell back to the runway, the left-wing digging into it. Then it righted itself and crashed back down on its main gear and went backwards down the runway until the engine quit. I ran out to see if the pilot was okay. He answered that he was. I asked him what happened. He replied, "I didn't lock my seat in a fixed position. When I took off, the seat slid backward and I didn't let go of the control column which made the nose pitch up. And here I am."

Being part of the world of aviation can create odd instances. Such as...the $64,000 question: Can a dead person who kills two people be tried for murder? Huh?

Since Metro was a fully operating airport, it meant that there were a lot of transient aircraft landing for fuel en route to another destination. One evening a C-172 landed and taxied to the ramp. After I showed the pilot where to park, he shut the engine down and two men dressed in black emerged. The pilot stood about 6 feet 5 inches tall. The other man was about 5 feet 2 inches. They were a real Mutt and Jeff couple. The pilot instructed me to fill the fuel tanks while they took a break to use the restroom. He then said, "Oh, and don't let our cargo get away."

I looked inside and noticed that the back seat was missing. Also missing was the leather shield that separated the passenger compartment from the back of the aircraft, where the control cables that move the elevator and the rudder are located. In its place was a body bag.

The pilot told me they were transporting a young woman who had been killed in an auto accident in Chicago to her home down near the Texas-Mexican border but would have to make one more fuel stop before getting to their destination.

Two days later, I read about an aircraft accident that killed two guys who were transporting a body. The authorities, according to the newspaper article, surmised that on take-off, the body bag slid backward into the tail section, making it tail heavy, thereby pitching the nose up at a higher-than-normal angle that the pilot couldn't overcome. Another theory was that the body became entangled with the control cables. Whatever the reason, the plane crashed, killing both men. Was it the same two guys? I was never sure, but I believe it was.

Most civilian airports have an advisory service called a Unicom in their flight operation office. Metro did as well. It transmitted and received on 122.8 MHz. An approaching aircraft could be given the active runway, wind direction, and velocity, like for commercial airports, but not take-off or landing instructions.

Several nights after the last incident, while I was working in the flight operations office, waiting for my shift to end, I heard someone transmitting on that frequency. He was lost, running low on fuel, and needed help.

Normally, in a case like that, the pilot would dial in 121.5, the emergency frequency all control towers are required to monitor, and ask them for help. In this situation, he didn't, and it happened to be one of those nights that was as black as the ace-of-spades. I ran outside and looked up, but saw nothing. Then I heard the sound of an aircraft engine way off in the distance. I ran back inside, grabbed the microphone, and told him to turn on his landing lights. I then ran back outside.

In the distance, I could see landing lights coming from the same direction as where I had heard the engine noise. I quickly ran back inside and turned up our runway lights to full bright.

The pilot told me he sees the runway. After he landed and parked the aircraft, he got out, shook my hand, and wanted to know where the bathroom was. He reeked of alcohol. Most likely, I saved his life.

One nice thing about having a Private Pilot's License is that you can carry passengers. My first passenger was Barbara. We flew up to Alton Airport in Alton Illinois where Walston had another flight office. We had lunch and flew back. It was great.

One of our customers who had a tie-down spot, aircraft that were not kept in a hangar, but on the ramp, asked if I would fly with him to a grass-strip airport about forty miles away. He wanted me to drop him off and bring the aircraft back to Metro. It just so happened his aircraft was a Luscombe, similar to the one I flew in Maine, and that was why he let me fly it. We flew over the open countryside, looked down at the farmlands, and spotted cows and horses grazing. It all seemed peaceful and quiet.

On the way back, far away from the airport I just departed, I dropped down to tree-top height, to see what it felt like skimming above them. My next bad idea was to buzz the cows and horses I had seen on the way over. They ran in all directions. A couple of the horses jumped fences and I'm pretty sure the cows weren't about to give any milk that night. Then I started worrying. What if someone saw me and took the registration number that is displayed in big block letters and numbers under the left wing and on top of the right wing of all aircraft? It would be "goodbye pilot's license."

Luckily nobody reported it. I learned my lesson.

The Metro had a large hangar that housed several corporate aircraft. Because I worked as a line boy for many months, I got to know several corporate pilots. They were very helpful in answering any questions I had about flying. One of them flew a twin-engine Piper Apache that had "Sweet Loraine" painted on its nose. The other flew a twin-engine Beechcraft Bonanza B-50. Part of my job was to clean those aircraft and fuel them when needed. The pilots often let me sit in the cockpits and explained the instrumentation. I couldn't wait to fly one of these planes.

Denny, who flew the B-50, was a retired Army Air Force pilot who had ferried many types of airplanes all over the world during World War II. He was very helpful when I asked him about different things that could happen while flying. I still remember the last question I asked him the night before he took off on a flight in the morning of December 4, 1958 with his employer. "What do you do if the weather unexpectedly turns bad while you are flying?" He told me he usually would try to get as low as he could under the clouds, so he wouldn't have to go on instruments. But, if he had to, he would call air traffic control and file an instrument flight plan.

Later that night, while they were returning to our Metropolitan Airport, the weather turned bad: rain, fog, and low visibility.

The following morning, I heard he crashed into a mountain south of the airport trying to get under the weather, killing himself and his passenger.

I was beginning to learn more about the responsibilities of being a pilot. Most people who make mistakes can erase them with an eraser. But sometimes, a pilot gets erased by his own mistakes. A day after I took my second flight instruction on how to fly on instruments, February 3, 1959, would become the day known as "The Day the Music Died."

The deaths of Buddy Holly, Richie Valens, and J.P. "The Big Bopper" Richardson in an airplane crash stunned the music world. The aircraft, a single-engine, V-tail, Beech Bonanza, they chartered, took off in marginal weather. There were snow squalls from Clear Lake, Iowa, all the way en route to Moorhead, Minnesota. The plane crashed just six miles from its point of departure. It was discovered later that the pilot was not qualified to fly on instruments. Their loss was immortalized by songwriter/singer Don McLean, best remembered for his song, "American Pie." It was a tribute to these three who died tragically in that crash.

My thought at the time was that those three guys in the Bonanza were trusting someone, the pilot, whom they believed was qualified to fly on instruments, but wasn't. Denny and his employer, who was qualified to fly on instruments, failed to use them. Both of these incidents made a big impression on me.

A week later, on February 10, 1959, there was another tragedy. It was

Mother Nature at her worse.

The cottage we lived in was very close to railroad tracks and you could hear the trains chugging along with an occasional blast of their whistle, but never in the middle of the night. Around 2:30 a. m., Barb and I awoke to what we thought was a runaway train barreling down the tracks. The cottage was shaking so badly that we thought the train had jumped off its track and was heading straight for us. We jumped out of bed and raced to the door and cautiously stepped outside. Nothing. The sound finally vanished, and we went back to bed.

When I arrived at the Metro that morning, I learned that a tornado struck the city of St. Louis in the middle of the night, causing extreme damage. Twenty-one people were killed, and over three hundred were injured.

One of our customers who stowed their airplane at the Metro was St. Louis's radio station WKWK. They owned a C-172 which they used for broadcasting traffic and weather conditions during the morning and evening rush hour. Bill Ryan, their pilot, whom I knew, had taken off into a low misty overcast sky, flying underneath it as he headed for downtown St. Louis to make his reports. Twenty minutes later, I heard the roar of an airplane engine and looked toward St. Louis. It was Ryan returning. He was getting lower and lower as he made his approach for what appeared to be a downwind landing. That is a "no, no," when the wind comes from behind you on your landing. He was still at full power when he touched down, hit the runway hard, bounced back into the air, flared, and touched down again. He was braking hard to avoid running off the end of the runway. He taxied to the ramp with brakes smoking, killed the engine, and got out of the plane. The leading edge of the wings, the horizontal stabilizer, the vertical stabilizer, wing struts, and wheel struts were covered with nearly an inch of clear ice created by low temperatures, and dangerous wet conditions.

In short, ice disrupts the aerodynamic flow of air over the wings, and if severe enough, the aircraft could stall. These conditions could also cause carburetor icing, and the engine might also quit. Had Ryan pulled the power back, he probably would have stalled and gone down. Luckily, he knew what to do.

In 1959, the Metropolitan Airport shut down. No airport, no job.

30

DETOURS

With the shutting down of Metro, I was out of a job. My flight training was still ongoing at Parks, so I needed to find work. I was determined to do whatever it took to become a flyer. Sometimes, it took a lot.

I read an advertisement in the newspaper for a job in St. Louis and took it. It lasted one day. The commute to St Louis was going to cost me more in gas, and tolls, than I was going to make.

The next job I tried was selling waterless cookware, pots, and pans. That went nowhere fast. The salesman who was teaching me how to sell these things was a very nice gentleman. However, he had one problem. His eyes. One went one way, the other, another. You couldn't help but notice it when you looked at him. His eyes were a major distraction.

The major selling point of the product was that you could take one drop of water from an eye-dropper, squeeze the drop between the lid and top of the pot, seal the cooker, and have precise waterless cooking. I had to demonstrate this to a couple in their home. My boss was with me but let me do it. I was nervous. After telling the potential customers all the good qualities of having waterless cookware, the time came for me to squeeze that one drop of water onto the cookware and seal it. I leaned over, the husband leaned over, the wife leaned over, and my boss leaned over, to watch me place this one drop. I squeezed the eyedropper so hard, its contents squirted the husband square in his eye, nearly blinding him. I knew then and there, I was never going to be a salesman. It was on to another job.

Lewis Matthis Steel Company in East St. Louis made copper tubing. My hourly pay went from $1.00, as a line boy, to $2.85, a percentage of which went to pay union dues. What's a union? I would soon find out.

It was, hard, hard, dirty, work. Steel-toed shoes were a requirement. You needed them for protection. The plant was extremely noisy, to the point that if you wanted to talk to someone, you had to stand right next to them, cup your hands to his ear, and shout as loud as you could to be heard.

My job was to cut 60-foot lengths of ½-inch tubing into 20-foot lengths of pipe using an automated cutting saw. The job was boring but paid well. There were accidents and people got hurt. The pipes were piled up in storage bins after you cut them. When the bin was full, an overhead crane would ride across on a rail and its operator would drop a hook. Thick hemp rope around the tubing would be attached to the hook, and a thumbs up would be given to the crane operator. He would sound an alarm that could be heard throughout the plant. Then everyone would get out of the way as the crane picked up the load and slowly moved it to the end of the building to a waiting truck. From there it went to a sorting area, where other workers would prepare the tubing for shipment.

Sometimes the crane operator would haul the tubing up too abruptly. The rope would snap under the weight and these twenty-foot lengths of pipes would come spilling down like spears. Guys would dive under tables, machines, and each other, to get out of the way. It was very dangerous.

One day a higher-paying job opened up and I applied for it. Fortunately for me, someone who was hired a day before me got it.

His job was to make sure the molten copper that came out of the mold in a cylindrical form rolled into a V-shaped slot. Once the cylinder was secure in the slot, he operated a press that exerted thousands of pounds of pressure and forced that molten copper into 60-foot lengths of tubing. A few days after he got the job, the cylinder came down sideways, as it often did. When that happened, the worker would use a metal peavey-pole that had a large metal hook on its end to push or pull on the cylinder until it slid into the slot correctly. This day, he was having trouble getting it positioned and went to step over the molten copper. No one was quite sure whether the safety mechanism failed, or he accidentally bumped the switch, but the press released and rammed into his right leg, severing it. He lost his balance, and the stump of his leg struck the molten copper, cauterizing it. That probably saved him from bleeding to death. The nineteen-year-old survived, but was now minus his right leg. I was lucky I did not get that job.

Thirty days later, the plant's union workers, including me, went on strike. Several days after the strike started, walking the picket line, with no pay and needing money for my flying lessons, I thought of crossing the picket line. I asked an older, hard-core guy, who stood six feet four and looked like he could play left tackle for the New York Giants, and had worked there for many years, what would happen if someone crossed a picket line. He looked me straight in the eye and his answer was short. "How well can you swim at the bottom of the Mississippi River with your feet encased in cement and your body wrapped in chains?"

It took me only a moment to realize he wasn't kidding. It was also the last time I went picketing, and I never did get back to work.

Barbara was supporting both of us. Fortunately, my flight training was coming to an end. But before taking my commercial pilot check-ride I had to begin the process of obtaining my multi-engine rating.

Parks used a twin-engine Cessna T-50 for their multi-engine rating test training. The T-50 was also called the UC-78 "Bobcat," affectionately known as the "Bamboo Bomber." During the early 1950s, there was a television program called *Sky King* starring Kirby Grant. He flew a "Bamboo Bomber," which he called the "Songbird." How I used to wish I could fly it.

Parks' T-50, N9803H, had two 225 HP Jacob Engines that cruised at 195 mph and had a service ceiling of approximately 22,000 feet. The plane could hold four passengers, plus the pilot. The reason they called it the "Bamboo Bomber" was that it was made of wood, tubular steel, and fabric.

My first lesson in it with Charles Gaedig was memorable. I started the number one engine, the left engine, and the cockpit began filling up with smoke. I'm thinking, we caught fire, this thing is going up in flames.

I unstrapped my seat belt and headed for the door.

Charles grabbed me by the seat of my pants to keep me from leaving, saying, "That's normal for these Jacob Engines."

Sure enough, each time we started the engines, in would come the smoky exhaust. After this first experience, I stayed in my seat, but with a keen eye toward the exit. When the smoke dissipated, away we would go.

The T-50 was enjoyable to fly, except for the "engine-out" maneuvers. Mr. Gaedig would fail the left engine on take-off. Throughout my career on any multi-engine aircraft that I was being trained on, it was always the left engine flight instructors would fail. Once the engine quit, you would have to push hard on the right rudder pedal to keep the aircraft straight and not have it yaw to the left. Why? "P-factor."

Here's a simple explanation. On take-offs, the aircraft is at a high angle of attack and slow speed. The propeller blades' P-factor (you have to remember a propeller has two blades) strikes the air at a different angle of attack. The descending blade produces more thrust, while the ascending blade has decreased thrust. Couple that with the failing engine producing more drag, the aircraft tends to turn toward the dead engine. Left. In cruise, the blades have an equal angle of attack thus no yaw. This comes into play, especially at the most critical phase of flight, the take-off. If you don't correct the turn, you may lose control of the aircraft and crash.

On August 18, 1959, I passed my check ride. I now had a multi-engine rating. After all the detours, I passed my first challenge.

Next up would be my commercial pilot rating.

31

SUCCESS & DISAPPOINTMENT

Having already passed my written test for the commercial pilot's license, all that was required would be to take a pre-rating check ride. Charles Gaedig signed me off to take it, which meant he thought I was ready to become a commercial pilot. But the rules state you had to take the pre-rating check ride with another flight instructor before doing the actual flight check. This had to be done by either an FAA inspector or a qualified flight examiner designated by the FAA. Guess who was going to give me that pre-rating check ride?

Charlie Parish.

We took off and did all the air work that was required: stalls, steep turns, etc. Then we came back and did the landings. Two landings you have to do are called a "360 overhead," one to the left, and the other to the right.

We did the first one to the left, landed, and went up again to do the right 360. I started the right 360, and Charlie comes unglued, ranting and raving. "Why are you doing a right 360 when you can see the runway better by doing a left 360?"

Now I'm thinking, is this a trick? They don't want me to do a right 360 because of the limited visibility. So, I bank the aircraft to the left, complete the 360, and land.

Surprisingly, Charlie signs me off.

Bob Phipps, the head of the flight department, was a certified flight examiner and would be the one who would give me the final check ride. I took the necessary oral exam, which went well, and then take off in the C-170 to do the air work. I do the left 360 overhead with no problems. We land and take off again to complete the check ride. Mr. Phipps says, "Okay, do the right 360."

I'm thinking this is another trick, part of the check ride, and he actually wants me to do a left one, like when Charlie Parish went bonkers. Instead of doing the right one, I do a left one again. Mr. Phipps says nothing. We land and go into his office. He starts with, "your check ride was perfect, except I asked you to do a right 360 and you didn't. You did a left. Why?"

Now, I'm worried. Did I fail my ride? Then I told him what happened with Parish. He shakes his head and says, "I'll be talking with Mr. Parish. Congratulations on becoming a commercial pilot," and he ups my grade.

I received my Commercial Pilot certificate on August 27, 1959. It was something for which both Barbara and I worked very hard. The year and a half we spent at Parks was over and I could not wait to start submitting my applications to the airlines.

We moved back to New Jersey shortly after and began the process of applying to the airlines. At the time there were many. American, Eastern, National, Trans World Airlines, Pan American, and United were my top choices. The smaller airlines like Allegheny, Central, North Central, Lake Central, Mohawk, Northeast, Piedmont, and several others were down on my list. I wrote to all of them, asking for an application, then waited weeks before receiving any of them.

In the meantime, Barbara found a position as a secretary with the pharmaceutical company, Warner Chilcott, in Morris Plains, N.J., and I ended up working for RCA Records as a typist, in their Rockaway, N.J. office, less than a mile from where my brother Glenn and I had lived with the Brennan family.

Finally, all the applications I sent out, came back with a good luck letter attached. I was nowhere near their flight requirements. You needed x-number of flying hours, an instrument rating, multi-engine time, flight experience as a pilot, and 20/20 vision. Plus, at that time, the age cut-off limit was no older than 27, and you needed to be at least 5 feet 9 inches, or taller. I met the age, height, and vision requirements, but along with this disappointment came the news that airlines had stopped hiring.

I hated being cooped up in that 9 to 5 office. The people that I worked with were great. The job was boring, boring, boring. The only time I can remember any excitement in the office was when the door to our office opened and in walked my boss, Danny Laterrie, with Lou Monte. He introduced all of us to Mr. Monte and we all shook hands. It was the second time that I had the honor of meeting someone in the entertainment business. The other was Martha Raye.

Monte, at the time, was a well-known singer, and under contract with RCA Records. He had been invited to see how the operation of pressing and shipping his RCA records was done. He had many hit records. One of his most popular was "Lazy Mary", which is still sung during the seventh-inning stretch at the New York Mets stadium. The other, "Dominick, The Donkey," still graces the airways at Christmas time.

My dream career, flying, was going nowhere fast. The position at RCA Records wasn't paying enough, and I had no intention of staying a clerk or storekeeper again. I was at a crossroads and was not sure of what to do next.

My thoughts now focused on another career. If I couldn't fly, I still needed to have something that offered us security, and eventually retirement. I applied to get back into the Dover Post Office, and the Postmaster, Mike De Lorenzo, offered me a position. So, it was back to the post office to deliver mail. But I was still dreaming of piloting commercial airlines. But how could I make that dream come true?

32

FLIGHT CHECKS

The months were quickly ticking by, and I wasn't getting any younger. I was frustrated. It was Barbara who began insisting I become a flight instructor. My answer to that was always, "No way!"

However, the 4:00 a.m. wake-up to go to work with the Post Office was beginning to get to me.

Barbara and I had a small apartment on Spruce Street in Dover. It was right next to the Orchard Street Cemetery. While Barbara used the only car we had to drive to work, I would walk to the post office through the cemetery.

On those cold, and sometimes foggy mornings, still half-asleep, I would squeeze through an opening in the fence that guarded it, weave my way around the headstones, and then squeeze out the fence on the other side. One morning, the weather conditions were like the ones you often see in horror movies, such as Frankenstein, The Wolf Man, and The Mummy. It was cold, foggy, and with limited visibility.

Halfway through the cemetery, I began to hear moaning sounds as though they were coming from one of the graves.

I took a few more steps and the moaning got louder.

I stopped to listen and try to see through the thick fog to determine the source of the moans. I walked around a headstone and stumbled over a body.

Laying against the headstone was some old, drunk guy. He started moaning again and I asked him if he was okay.

He looked at me, took a swig from the bottle he was holding, nodded his head, fell asleep, and began snoring loudly.

I didn't know if he was a local guy or a hobo that might have hopped off a freight train that passed through the town.

Just two blocks from the cemetery were the main railroad tracks and the siding where boxcars, like the ones I used to play on, were parked. Next to the tracks were a couple of bars, that stayed open late at night, where you could buy alcohol, a pint, or a bottle, and take it with you. I checked him again. He sounded as if he was going to get a good night's sleep.

But I wasn't getting too much sleep, not with flying still on my mind.

With both of us now working, Barbara and I were able to save some of our income. Barbara kept insisting that I get a flight instructor's rating. My concern had always been that it was going to cost a lot of money to obtain that certification. I was afraid it might deplete all our savings. Finally, I relented, but only after another affectionate swift kick in the seat of my pants from my dear wife.

At the beginning of April 1961, I drove to Morristown Municipal Airport in Morristown, New Jersey, looking for a flight school. There were two of them there. One was in a small building just outside a fence that guarded the main body of the airport. The other was located inside one of the hangars inside the fence.

The outside flight school was in an older-looking building that appeared to have been there since the early forties. Inside its cramped office, there was a glass counter that held sectional maps, flight logs, books on flying, E-6B Computers used for flight navigation, plus a mix of other flight-related items. There was also a desk, a few chairs, and a coffee pot. The other flight school's office was large, clean, and had up-to-date furniture, with several large glass counters which also held the flight-required items. Flight instruction costs were about the same.

It was a no-brainer.

After talking to Chief Pilot, Walt "Sandy" Sanders, I decided that "Wings of Morristown," was the ideal flight school for me. It was the one on the

119

outside of the fence.

The flight instructors for "Wings" were very friendly and helpful in answering the slew of questions I had. The building reminded me of the one at Hackettstown Airport when I first started flying. It had the charm of those airplane movies I would sneak into when I was a kid. It reminded me of the movies where the pilots hung around in a beat-up flight operations office, often with their heads hanging down, lamenting the loss of one of their own, because of a crack-up, or where they were about to race out the door for some dangerous mission.

On April 4, 1961, I began my first lesson toward becoming a flight instructor. My instructor was Jesse McEwan. He always wore Khaki pants, brown shoes, a brown shirt, and an old Air Force windbreaker. Even the jeep he drove was air force blue. It was obvious he was once a pilot in the Air Force and was still proud of that. I enjoyed flying with Jesse. He was easy-going, and a very good instructor.

So began my quest for a flight instructor rating. And again, it was back to doing air work. That turned out to be similar to my commercial pilot's rating training but more advanced. I had to learn to make steep turns, lazy 8's, chandelle's, slow flights, loops, stalls, forced landings, spirals to landings, missed approaches, spot landings, short-field take-offs and landings, and spins. That was a lot to learn, but I was determined.

How do you get an aircraft to spin? Good question. Remember those old movie combat scenes where the aircraft is spinning out of control after being shot down?

All the actor-pilot did was bring the nose of the aircraft upward at a high angle of attack while holding full back-elevator pressure. When the aircraft stalled, he pushed full rudder pressure in the direction he wanted the aircraft to spin. When the nose dropped down, he maintained the backpressure and continued holding it until he wanted to come out of the spin. To do that, he released the backpressure, pushed forward on the control column so that the elevator neutralized, and at the same time pushed the opposite rudder to stop the spin and make the recovery.

As an instructor, I usually started my spins at about 3,000 feet. I'd count three full rotations, then make my recovery, at about 1,500 feet above the ground. I would do those only if the student wanted to be shown what it felt like. Not many did.

Jess and I would fly for several hours together. That would be followed by a flight check by Sandy as to my progress. Unfortunately, there were only so many hours a week I could devote to flying, since having to work for the post office five days a week.

The weather became another factor and flights were often canceled. Other cancelations occurred when my instructors weren't available on the days I could fly. So, on it went for four months. The cost was a big problem. The more flight hours, the deeper it was digging into our savings.

Despite all the problems, my flying hours were building up, and I had taken the FAA flight instructor's written exam and passed.

Shortly after the written test, it was time for my flight instructor's flight check. This was to be given by one of the FAA inspectors at Teterboro Airport, in Teterboro, New Jersey.

On August 7, 1961, with the recommendation in hand from Sandy, I flew to Teterboro Airport in one of our C-150s and met with FAA Inspector, Dick Claus.

After introductions, it became apparent that if I were to become a flight instructor, I better damn well know how to instruct. And, I better damn well know about sectional charts, and about the aircraft about which I would instruct my students. He was thorough, but I was prepared.

After the quiz ended, it was time for the flight check.

We took off and headed for the practice area where I did all the required air work that Jesse and Sandy taught me.

An hour and a half later, we landed and I followed Mr. Claus to his office. I wondered if I passed. It had been such a long struggle. Barbara had sacrificed so much. Was it for nothing?

Mr. Claus looked at me and smiled. "Congratulations. You are now a certified flight instructor."

I couldn't believe it. I couldn't wait to tell Barbara.

I flew back to "Wings," and told Sandy I passed. I began to thank him for all of his help. Before I could finish, he said, "I like the way you fly and handle an airplane. How would you like a job here at Wings as one of our flight instructors?"

I jump at the chance and give my two weeks' notice at the post office.

Next up, I had to meet the owner of "Wings," Chet Smiley. I hoped he would be as enthusiastic about me as Sandy was.

33

THE TRAINER

C het Smiley stood about five foot seven. He was sort of stocky, had grey hair, a mustache, and smoked cigars. He would normally be wearing black pants, black shoes, white shirts, a black fedora, and dark sunglasses. I was an instructor at "Wings" for three years and I don't remember him dressing any other way.

Chet also owned an electronics company in Montgomery, Pennsylvania, where he lived, although I believe "Wings" was his primary passion. He would fly to Morristown a couple of times a week to see how things were progressing, and check the number of charters we flew, and the number of new students that took advantage of our flight training program. I enjoyed working for him...most of the time.

The pay wasn't much. Sixty dollars a week as a new flight instructor, plus, two dollars per hour for the first ten hours you taught, and then three dollars per hour after that. Each week the cycle would begin again.

"Wings" had several flight instructors who were considered full-time employees. Our Chief Pilot, Walt "Sandy" Sanders, Jesse McEwan, Nancy McMurray, and George Oaks. Several other part-time instructors would fill in occasionally.

On August 8, 1961, I had my first student. A forty-five-minute familiarization flight with Mr. Sam Jaffe (not the actor) in aircraft N7199X. "Wings" had many introductory offers, and most of the time the people who took advantage of them signed up for flying lessons.

Normally, we would recommend only a one-hour lesson for new students. More than that, it seemed their learning curve spiraled downward. Several days later I was asked to take over one of our part-time instructor's students. The instructor found out he had terminal throat cancer from smoking and would not be back. He died shortly after.

One of my students, Bob Patten, was a seventeen-year-old lad who had quite a few flying hours to his credit and was doing rather well.

I flew with him for two one-hour sessions, then came the third. At the time Morristown Airport had two runways in operation. Runway 5/23 was approximately 6,000 feet long and runway 13/31 was 4,000 feet long.

On August 11, 1961, we were practicing take-offs and landings on runway 5. What little wind existed was straight down the runway. We did two landings to a full stop in aircraft N7791E. As we taxied back to do another take-off, I told him to stop and let me out. A smile spread across his face, then his expression turned serious when he realized it would be his first solo.

I stepped out of the plane and gave him a good-luck salute. Then I stood in the grass near the end of the runway. I don't know who was more apprehensive, him or me. It was his first solo and it was my first time to let someone go solo.

He took off, came around, and made a perfect landing. Then he came back down the taxiway to pick me up. I motioned for him to do two more full-stop landings. This is an FAA requirement before an instructor will allow the student to fly without a flight instructor. There was a bigger grin on his face than before. Mine too. I would see those kinds of grins each time I soloed someone.

From that moment on, whatever thoughts I might have had of the "what-ifs," if something goes wrong during any of my students flying solo, were gone. I knew I trained them right and they were ready.

I began instructing six days a week, from eight in the morning to nightfall. I would fly an hour, get out of the two-seat Cessna 150 we used for training, grab a cup of coffee and a snack, get back in with the next student, and off we'd go.

The weather was always a large factor. We had many cancellations due to thunderstorms. Sometimes, it was too windy, foggy, or cloud ceilings were too low. The one factor that I always taught my students: "First and paramount is safety first."

Safety began with the pre-flight inspection of the aircraft. Check the amount of oil in the engine. Check the amount of fuel onboard, both by the fuel gauges and a finger check of the gas tanks which were located on top of the C-150 wings. Other checks included checking for dents in the wings, the vertical stabilizer, the horizontal stabilizer, the rudder, and wing struts.

Then came the flight controls. Pull back on the control column to see if the elevator is pointing up, then push forward to see if the elevator is pointing down. This determines whether the aircraft will climb or descend. The ailerons: turn the control column to the left for a left turn, the left aileron points up, the right points down; and to the right just the opposite. Why do all these flight control checks? You are making sure your aircraft is airworthy.

When training any of my new students, I always began with a walk-around inspection of the aircraft. One time while I was explaining all of this to one of my new female students, I placed my hand on the propeller and said, "Ginny, let's talk about the P-factor." Before I could say anything else, she replied, "Don't worry about that. I went to the potty before I came here."

I flew many hours with Ginny before she soloed. After a few more hours of solo flight, we began cross-country flight planning.

As I stated before, I always used the TVMDC method for planning a cross-country flight. Without thinking, I began my "True Virgins Make Dull Companions" dissertation on planning a cross-country flight. Her comment to that was, "I'm not a virgin."

Ginny excelled in grasping each process of our flight curriculum and went on to obtain her private pilot's license. I was glad to be part of her success.

One of the misconceptions people who are not familiar with aircraft have is one I often hear about: "The engine stalled." Engines and motors don't stall. They quit! Airplane's stall. Case in point. You've thrown, or seen someone throw a toy balsa wood airplane into the air. It goes nose-high, stops, then the nose pitches down, gains airspeed, pitches up, and the sequence begins again. In that nose-high attitude, the balsa wood airplane stalled. It's no different from a real aircraft. If the aircraft does not have enough airspeed, the aircraft stalls.

Practicing stalls are part of the training process. Why? Because when you make your landings, you should be at or near your stall speed just before touching down. The aircraft we used to instruct in was the C-150. During my tenure as a flight instructor, I would show my students, at altitude, stalls. Of course, they would also have to perform and recover from them. And they would have to perform stalls when they flew solo as part of obtaining a pilot's certificate.

I was racking up many flight hours toward what the airlines required. At the same time, I was working on obtaining the instrument flight rating that the airlines required. Jess McEwan and Nancy McMurray were the two instrument flight instructors who would help me obtain it. Then came the Death Spiral.

34

THE DEATH SPIRAL AND THE ACTOR

Remember a spiral is not a spin. There is a major difference between the two: airspeed. In a spin, your airspeed is relatively low. But in a "graveyard spiral," your airspeed is fast and increasing. You can, if trained, recover from a spin. The spiral can be more deadly. I will demonstrate.

Look at your watch. Second hand at twelve. But this time, you do not have two minutes, just 90 seconds. Start the second hand.

You've just taken off and climbed a few hundred feet into instrument conditions. You immediately find that you lost the reference to the ground and the horizon. You look outside the cockpit searching for something that tells you where you are. Nothing. But you think you are climbing straight and your wings are level in the climb, but most likely you are already in a slight turn to the left, roll because of that P-Factor. The roll rate continues to increase since the lift of the airplane's axis is no longer vertical to support the aircraft as in straight and level flight. You look at your instruments. The airspeed indicator, your altimeter. Even though you know what they tell you, you begin to make what you believe is the right correction. Your instinct tells you to pull back on the control column to get the nose up to bleed off the airspeed and gain altitude. That's when you realize the nose of the aircraft is beginning to point down. Your heart rate begins to increase because you've now developed the so-called "fear factor," panic. The airspeed increases, the altitude plummeting. The more you pull back, the further the nose drops. The spiral becomes steeper, tighter. You break out of the clouds. The ground is rushing up to meet you. You pull back harder. Too late. Your 90 seconds are up.

Unfortunately, this does happen. All too often. Still, you might have departed from an airport where the weather is CAVU, Ceiling and Visibility Unlimited, but failed to check your en-route weather or the weather at your intended destination. You fly into instrument conditions, become disoriented, start spiraling, and down you go.

I always taught my students if ever they begin to encounter marginal weather conditions, do what we were all taught to do. Do a 180 turn around and go back to where you came from.

Over the next few years, I helped men and women obtain their private, commercial, instrument, and multi-engine pilot licenses and was very happy for them. Of course, some others just couldn't grasp the art of flying.

When I wasn't instructing, I would be doing air-charters. I enjoyed it because they were a change from constant take-off and landings, and doing air work with my students.

On November 25, 1961, I flew a charter from Morristown to Manchester, Vermont, in our Cessna Skyhawk N8199X. The Skyhawk is a four-passenger aircraft, but this day there was only one passenger, a Mr. Ed Hallock. The weather was CAVU all the way, the air smooth as silk until I started letting down for my approach and landing at Manchester. We just crossed over the area of the Big Equinox Mountain Ridge which is approximately 3800 feet above sea level when we got slammed by what I thought was a mountain wave.

For several moments, the instruments were a blur. The shock was so severe, that I thought the wings were going to snap off. Then the wind was gone. I checked my instruments and saw my vertical speed indicator glass cover was shattered. The vertical needle was stuck in its max climb position. Had we not been wearing our seat belts, I believe we both would have hit the ceiling and broken our necks. We landed without any other incident. While my passenger left for his business meeting, I solicited a mechanic and had him check for structural damage. After his inspection, he told me everything appeared to be normal. Our flight back to Morristown was uneventful, but a lot more cautious. I took the long way around the mountain. Bill Hasselbeck, our mechanic, made another structural check. He also said all was well and replaced the vertical speed indicator.

I later learned that glider pilots often used the Equinox Mountain Ridge for soaring. Sometimes gliders rose to tens of thousands of feet just by riding those mountain waves and updrafts.

Several days after that last episode, November 29, 1961, I took my instrument flight check at Teterboro with FAA Inspector J.A. Twaddell in aircraft N6559T. I passed! This was a milestone for me. I now had three of the four requirements airlines required: a commercial pilot's license, a multi-engine rating, and now, an instrument pilot's rating. The only thing left was to get enough flight time.

Vic Quinto was a student I began instructing on November 4, 1961. He already held a private pilot license and was now training for a commercial pilot license. He also wanted a flight instructor rating. I would help him obtain both. He would become one of Wings' flight instructors.

Another student of mine was Richie Green. I also helped him obtain both a commercial and flight instructor rating. He also became an instructor for "Wings." Both became good friends.

Part of the training before becoming a commercial pilot requires X number of hours of logged **night** flight time. Night flying is a lot different than daytime. There are a limited number of reference points, such as the "Iron Compass," railroad tracks. Highways and towns that are visible during the daytime are hidden in the black of night, except for automobile headlights or street lights.

At night, most navigation is done by visual flight rules (VFR) or the VOR navigational aid. Still, you must be always cognizant of where you are. Even seasoned pilots have been known to get lost by not paying attention. "The airplane doesn't know if it's day or night."

In December 1961, Nancy and Jess would take turns, depending on their flight schedules, to help me get checked out to fly our twin-engine

Piper Apache N3044P that we used for charter flying. It had two 160 HP Lycoming engines, cruised at 150 mph, held 72 gallons of fuel, had a range of approximately 600 miles, a ceiling of 17,000 feet, and a stall speed of only 53 mph. It could carry up to six passengers, including the pilot.

I did quite a few charter flights in that aircraft, including to an airport named Idlewild, now called JFK.

One of the many charters I flew in 44P was for Robert Vesko. The first was on February 13, 1962. Jess and I had flown to Nantucket, Massachusetts, where Vesko was staying. Then flew he and his family back to Morristown. Little did I realize what was to transpire in the years to come for him and the business world.

Robert Vesko would become an American criminal financier. After years of risky investments and dubious credit dealings, Vesco was alleged to have committed securities fraud by the U.S. Securities and Exchange Commission. He then fled the country. He would eventually end up in a Cuban jail charged with drug smuggling.

Through our newspaper advertisements and word of mouth, Wings was becoming well known as the best flight school in the Morris County area.

In May of 1962, one of my new students was Bob Leamy. After several hours of instruction, he told me he worked for the Wild Film Studio in New York City, producing television commercials for many major companies. After one of our sessions, he asked me if I would be his pilot for a night flight to film Coney Island's Amusement Park. This was to be used for a Carlings Black Label Beer segment. Of course, I said yes. We took off and headed for Coney Island. When we arrived, I dropped down to a couple of hundred feet above the Atlantic Ocean and then proceeded to fly up and down the beach as he filmed the park. That segment appeared in the commercial.

There were several other occasions when Leamy filmed commercials using our aircraft, myself as the pilot. One of the commercials was for Firestone Tires. This one used Al Luciano, one of my students, in the commercial. Al owned a farm in New Jersey and had an old John Deere Tractor he used and had just put new Firestone tires on it. The commercial showed Al bouncing along on his tractor with a close-up of his new Firestone Tires. That ad ran for several weeks.

Then came the chance for me to be in an L & M Cigarette commercial. Bob and his Wild Films partner gathered several of our flight instructors around one of our C-150s. They took numerous photos and films of us sitting in the airplane or standing next to the propeller smoking an L & M Cigarette. After reviewing the results, they decided the person who would be chosen for the commercial should be older with a touch of grey hair.

Jesse McEwan got the part. The ad showed him sitting in the C-150 smoking an L & M Cigarette while looking skyward. The commercial was about thirty seconds long and was shown often during the following six weeks. Being in a commercial was quite lucrative for Jess. Every time it ran, he received a royalty, which came to be several thousand dollars over the six weeks it played. Good for him. For me? My chances of being an actor went up in a puff of smoke.

35

LESSONS LEARNED

My experience as a flight instructor made me realize that most students required more than the minimum 40 hours of flight training required by FAA Part 61 before being ready to apply for a private pilot's certificate.

Many of our students would take a one-hour lesson, once a week, then they might miss several weeks. In the interim, what was learned previously might be virtually forgotten. Learning to fly isn't like driving an automobile, where you jump in your car, start the engine, and drive off.

One week away from a student flying and instructors might have to review some of what we believed they had learned. Then there were weather cancellations, financial problems, illness, and just some students that were slow to grasp what we taught. The list of obstacles goes on and contributed to needing more flight hours for some students. I believe the average student, at that time, took approximately 50 to 60 hours of flight time before we could recommend they take their FAA flight check for their private pilot's license.

Part of the training was to teach the student how to handle unforeseen emergencies, such as engine failure in flight. Sometimes it requires steel nerves by the instructor to sit there judging how far you can allow a student to proceed before you take over control of the aircraft.

Our in-flight practice area was nearby, over Boonton Reservoir, Boonton, New Jersey. Several other small grass-field airports were in that area:

Boonton Radio Corporation Airport, Towaco Airport, and Totowa-Wayne Airport. On this day, my student was doing so well that I pulled the throttle back to idle, to simulate an engine failure. I asked him where he was going to land. He spied Lincoln Park Airport and started his glide toward the field. One thing you don't want to do is try to stretch your glide to make the field. Don't slow the airplane to the point where you keep pulling the nose of the aircraft up trying to make the field. All you will do is stall and bury the nose into the ground. You're better off landing in trees under control and walking away.

As we were making our approach, I thought we were getting a little low, but he had the airspeed, and I knew we were okay to land. He landed without incident. As we began to taxi back for take-off, a man came out of the nearby flight shack and walked directly in front of my airplane, stopping only a few feet from my spinning propeller. I killed the engine, not sure if this guy had a death wish. He yelled at me to come into his office and sign the register. Perplexed, I killed the engine, got out of the airplane, and wanted to know why he stopped us.

It turns out the man was Mr. Ed Gorski, the owner and operator of the airport. According to him, our engine failure was a little too realistic. People were calling saying they saw our aircraft flying so low that they thought it was going to crash.

I told Mr. Gorski that I had a student and we were practicing forced landings and everything was under control. He insisted I sign the register, which I did. He then ordered me off his airport and said I was never to come back.

Back at Morristown, I informed Sandy of what took place and then called FAA's Dick Klaus to let him know. Nothing ever came from it. However, there were no more instructional landings at Lincoln Park Airport.

At the time I did not know who Mr. Ed Gorski was, nor do I remember anyone ever telling me other than that he owned Lincoln Park Airport. Shortly after our encounter, I found out who he was and his place in the early years of aviation.

Ed Gorski and Bernt Balchen were Amelia Earhart's chief mechanics. They prepared her Lockheed Vega 5B, which she nicknamed "Bessie," for her solo trans-Atlantic flight. On May 20, 1932, she took off from Harbour Grace, Newfoundland. 14 hours and 58 minutes later, she landed in Londonderry, Ireland. Her Vega 5B now sits in the National Air and Space Museum in Washington, D.C.

Several days after that incident, I experienced a real engine failure. One of my students belonged to a flying club. Their club owned a C-140, a two-seat tail dragger, and used us as their instructors. My student had one bad habit. That was to ram the throttle to full power instead of applying it smoothly each time we practiced stall recovery or go-around procedures.

On this particular practice stall occasion, he rammed in the throttle. I pulled it back to idle and told him the engine just failed. "Where are you going to land?"

It just so happened, we were doing the air work near Basking Ridge Airport, a small grass field. Since we had a lot of altitude, he had time to set up his glide and he approached the runway but was higher than he should have been to make the landing, even if he tried slipping the aircraft which pilots often do to lose altitude and not gain airspeed. (Wing down and slightly cross-control aileron/rudder.) He said he could make it. I said, "I don't think so. Go around!"

I could see he was upset because I wouldn't let him land. With that, he rammed the throttle into full power. A loud clunk sound came from the engine, and it started to lose power. I took control of the airplane and began looking for a place to land. The only open area ahead of me was a schoolyard, but kids were playing in it. I couldn't land there.

Fortunately, the engine was holding what power it still had. We were less than a hundred feet in the air as I eased into a slow descending turn back toward the runway. The engine was still sputtering as I turned on our final approach, then it quit. The prop stopped turning.

We barely cleared the fence. I made a dead-stick landing and the plane rolled to a stop. Thankful we made the field, we got out and pushed the airplane off the runway to get it out of the way.

According to our mechanic, when my student rammed the throttle to full power, it caused both magnetos to shear and fail. Highly unusual. What are magnetos? I'll explain them in simple terms.

Magnetos are usually found in pairs on piston-driven aircraft. They supply high-power ignition electrical current to the spark plugs that fire up the engine. There are four positions of the switch you can select. The left magneto, the right, or as most pilots do, select the third position, on both. In the "off" position, the engine won't start or run.

Shortly after that incident came another close call.

I had a student who was a slow learner and I had given him many, many hours of flight instruction. He was still nowhere near ready to solo. Even a change of instructors did not seem to be the answer. In any event, I again became his instructor.

The C-150 we were to use had a dead battery. The procedure was to spin the prop by hand. That is, pull down hard on the propeller blade and stand clear as you do, so it won't take your hands or your head off when it roars to life. I told him to stay in the cockpit and keep his feet firm on the brakes while I pulled the propeller a couple of times.

"Brakes set. Switch off," I said, making sure that the magneto switch was in the off position so that the engine wouldn't start while I pulled on the prop.

"Brakes set. Switch off," he answered.

The airplane had low engine compression. That meant the engine could use a major overhaul. I put my hand on top of one side of the prop blade and my other hand on the bottom side. I spun it. The prop spun around several times. I called, "Gus, I'm going to pull the prop through one more time. Keep your feet firm on the brakes."

"Okay," came his reply.

Instead of turning the prop, I pulled down on it with both hands. The engine roared to life, the propeller nearly taking my hands off. He pushed the throttle making the propeller spin faster. I backed away from the flashing blades that were just inches from my face and dove to the ground. I rolled out of the way hoping he wouldn't release the brakes and run me over.

Shaken, I slid into the right seat and asked him what the hell was he thinking. He answered, "I thought you said, switches on."

I just shook my head and thanked my guardian angels again.

That wasn't the end of it.

The C-150 has a cramped cockpit, so I would normally drape my left arm on top of the seatback of students that had many hours of flight instruction. No sooner than we were about ten feet in the air when he reached for the magneto switch and turned it to the "off" position.

Because I had my arm behind his seat back, I couldn't reach the switch to turn it back on. The engine began sputtering and was about to quit. Here we were just above stalling speed when we slammed back down on the runway and narrowly ran off the end. The prop was still spinning and about to stop. I managed to get my arm around Gus and quickly put the switch back where it belonged. The engine caught and I taxied off the runway. The control tower personnel thought we had an emergency and were about to send out the crash trucks. I advised them all was okay, taxied back to the ramp, and shut down the engine.

Once safe, I asked Gus why he turned off the mags. He said he didn't think the engine would quit. I spent the next fifteen minutes trying to convince him he wasn't cut out to be a pilot. He asked for another chance. I relented but ended that day's session. After several more hours and no improvement, thankfully, he was convinced. Some people should not fly. Period.

Accidents happen when you least expect them.

One evening, just before sunset, I was returning to Morristown Airport after instructing a student on cross-country flying. As we turned on the final approach to runway 23, I noticed another aircraft a mile or so behind us. He appeared to be approaching the same runway. I then focused back on our landing.

After we landed safely, I looked back in the other plane's direction, but he was no longer in sight. I assumed he might be landing at Hanover Airport, just several miles from Morristown. I didn't give it another thought.

Two days later, I read in the newspaper, the pilot had crashed into a wooded area about a mile-and-a-half short of the runway we landed on. Out-of-gas. Thankfully, the aircraft didn't catch fire, no fuel, but he was busted up pretty badly and had to spend the rest of the night in the woods. The following morning, he somehow managed to crawl to a highway and flagged down a passing car whose driver drove him to a nearby hospital. He was lucky. Too many were not.

Being a full-time flight instructor, working six days a week, kept me busy. Between flight instruction and charter flying, the weeks, months, the year, went by rapidly. 1962 came and went. There were times when I thought my students were out to kill me. Usually, it came from them over-controlling the aircraft: too much rudder, too much aileron, too much elevator, too slow, too fast, indecision on knowing when you must abandon your approach and go around and try again. Oddly enough, I enjoyed it. I think it was part of that adventure, or daring, or that excitement of living on the edge, that was in me growing up. Whatever it was, my flight hours were building.

When I finally reached the minimum flight hours required for some of the airlines, out went the applications. Back came the rejections.

By that time, the airlines were looking more toward military pilots than civilian pilots, which wasn't helping me. In December of 1963, I would be twenty-seven, with only one more year of eligibility left. Here it was February 1963, and I was beginning to feel the time was running out. It was disheartening. Would I ever achieve my lifelong dream of becoming a commercial pilot?

36

THE BLACK CLOUD

At that time the Federal Air Regulations Part 61 stated that under an approved school and using their curriculum, the least amount of time required to obtain a private pilot's license was 35 hours.

Because of our popularity, and since we were an approved flight school, Chet was also able to get a contract with Seaton Hall University's Army ROTC flight program.

Each of those ROTC students was to be given 35 hours of flight training which was paid for by the government. However, if for some reason that person could not meet the required expectations in those 35 hours, he or she could continue to obtain the license at their own expense. Which, several of our ROTC students did.

The addition of having the ROTC group was good for our flight instructors. The more students, the more flight time, and the more pay. But my interest wasn't on the pay. My goal was on gaining more flight hours.

Generally, most of our students, whether they were ROTC or not, required more than thirty-five hours before they were ready to obtain a private pilot's license.

Once their ROTC program was completed, and after they graduated from Seaton Hall University, they were sent to Fort Rucker, Alabama. Once there, one group continued their fix-wing training program. The other group became helicopter pilots. Some were sent to Vietnam and flew many combat missions.

Two of my ROTC students would eventually fly for Eastern Air Lines. Another student of mine who was part of the initial group, and who was also being taught to fly by another instructor, was George Meade. Years later George would work for WOR Radio reporting morning rush hour traffic conditions for New York's Metropolitan area, in WOR'S traffic helicopter.

In February 1963 Chet informed us that he signed a contract to re-open Caldwell-Wright Airport and would be moving our entire flight operations there.

But several weeks before moving, things got a little too exciting. First, Chet told us if we had anything of value in the hangar, to get it out before morning. We did.

The hangar burnt down that night, destroying several aircraft inside. It seems a space heater that was being used to keep paint from jelling in the cold hangar caught fire in the middle of the night. Hmmm.

Another one of my students was a well-known judge in Morristown. You would think with his background he would have a lot of common sense. But a student pilot is a student pilot, and he nearly caused a calamity.

Sy had quite a few hours under his belt and had already soloed. On this day he was to go out solo and practice take-offs and landings. It snowed the night before and the runways and taxiways had been plowed. Both were clear of snow, but during the plowing, they left mounds of snow along their edges that stood nearly fifteen inches high.

The ramp where we parked our aircraft was directly across from a ramp that led to the Continental Cans ramp and its hangar. As Sy taxied away from our ramp, he saw a Continental Corporate aircraft coming down the taxiway toward him. He turned into the Continental Cans ramp with the corporate aircraft right behind him. The corporate parked and killed his engines which blocked Sy. He could not get around their aircraft.

No problem. Sy decided to taxi over the snow pile. He applied full power and got the nose wheel and the right main gear over the pile but did not get the left wheel over. He was stuck. Still. No problem. He got out of the aircraft, and instead of throttling back pushed upward on the left-wing strut to get the left wheel over.

Bill Hasselbeck, our mechanic, just happened to be outside our hangar and saw what was happening. He yelled to Sy to stop and raced for the aircraft. I heard the commotion and charged out of our office just in time to see Sy get the left main over the snow mound and then fall.

Bill leaned into the cockpit, his feet dragging along the ground, as the aircraft moved forward, and he killed the engine. By that time, it had crossed the taxiway and was heading straight for another aircraft parked on our ramp.

The snow mound on our side of the taxiway prevented our plane from hitting the other aircraft. If Bill did not react so quickly, there was a very good possibility Sy's aircraft would have gotten airborne without its pilot or might have crashed into other parked aircraft. It was an air disaster waiting to happen. Sy blamed it all on the aircraft that blocked him. We did several more hours of instruction before I let him go solo again. Along with a lesson on what not to do.

Shortly after that episode, our Chief Pilot, Walt Sanders, as all of our instructors did at one time or another, gave flight instructions to a group of people who had their own airplanes or belonged to a flying club. This day, he was asked by the owner of a Global-Swift airplane, a low-wing, all-metal airplane, built like a tank, for additional flight instructions.

They took off on runway 23, westbound, which was toward the city of Morristown. No sooner were they airborne when the engine sputtered and quit.

They crash-landed on top of a bunch of oak trees. The Swift came to rest nestled in the tree branches high above the ground. They climbed down unscathed. The cause of the crash: *Water in the fuel tank.*

Most airports have underground fuel storage tanks. Inside the tanks, the fuel, being lighter than water, lays at the top. There is always that possibility of condensation inside the tank, adding to the water already there. Sometimes, when the underground fuel tank is replenishing, usually from a fuel tanker, the pressure from filling the tank stirs the water and it mixes with the fuel. That's what happened in this incident. They fueled their aircraft shortly after the tank was replenished and received a mixture of fuel and too much water.

In early March 1963, we moved our entire flight operations to Caldwell-Wright Airport, well-known for its history and the men for whom the airport was named: The Wright Brothers and Glenn Hammond Curtis.

We all know about the historic feat the Wright Brothers achieved when their engine-driven Wright Flyer became airborne on December 17, 1903, at Kill Devil Hills, North Carolina. But few may remember Glenn Hammond Curtis.

Curtis was another one of those early pioneers of aviation. He had only a formal education through eighth grade. Many of the men who took to the skies in those early years had minimal education. He set many world records in motorcycle racing and flying machines. He also designed and manufactured aircraft engines for airships and aircraft. The Wright Brothers Aeronautical Corporation, and his Curtis Aeronautical Corporation, became the Curtis-Wright Corporation in 1929. Their company developed airframes, aircraft engines, propellers, and aircraft parts.

During World War II, the company manufactured many different types of aircraft. One was the P-40 Warhawk, which became well-known to the American public for building the planes used by General Claire Chennault's famed AVG group (the American Volunteer Group), best known as the Flying Tigers.

Curtis-Wright also produced the C-46 Commando, the navy SB2C Helldiver, and other essential aircraft for America. Their aircraft engines, such as the R-1820 and the R-3350, powered such heavy bombers as the B-17 and the B-29. They had affiliates spread throughout the eastern and central portions of the United States. Buffalo, Columbus, and St. Louis were all building aircraft. Cincinnati, Indianapolis, and Pittsburg manufactured propellers. Caldwell-Wright engines and propellers. Now, Wings of Morristown was being housed at this famous airport.

Our flight operations at Caldwell-Wright Airport began in early March 1963. At the time, the field had three operational runways and a control tower, which was not operating. That created some huge problems. A tetrahedron and a windsock were located between the runways to indicate which runway was the active runway.

Once it was known the airport was operational, the floodgates opened. Aircraft owners who had their aircraft based at Morristown, Teterboro, and other surrounding airports flocked there. Cheaper tie-down and hangar rates added to its attraction. As did having a restaurant that opened early and closed late, where many a pilot would linger telling tall tales.

At first, it was like a flying circus. Airplanes were all over the place, taking off and landing on the different runways, causing many near collisions. Hot-headed pilots almost got into fistfights when each thought they had the right of way. Eventually, things calmed down after notices were posted on bulletin boards about observing airport policies. But, for some unknown reason, there always seemed to be a black cloud, an omen, hanging over that airport. Unfortunately, it became the scene of fatal and non-fatal accidents in the months to come. And I would be in the middle of that black cloud.

37

THE CELEBRITY

"Wings" beefed up our advertising. Introductory flight packages were offered, our best way of drawing in more students. The one drawback to our training program was there was no active control tower to teach our students the basic use of the aircraft's radios. So, it would be back to Morristown Airport for that practice.

Not having an operating control tower created additional problems. Notably, other flight schools, from other airports, would bring their students to our field to practice take-offs and landings. They wanted to avoid the delays of having to wait in line to take off or land as they had at airports such as Morristown and Teterboro.

Just when you thought everything at our field was under control, back came the flying circus. Most of the problems concerned getting into, or out of, the traffic pattern. It required keeping a sharp eye to avoid a mid-air collision.

One of our flight instructors' responsibilities, along with the supervision of airport maintenance and mechanics personnel, was knowing how to operate the airport's sole fire truck. The truck was a 1950's vintage American La France 4X4 crash truck. We needed it in the event of a grass fire where our aircraft were tied down or worst, an accident involving an aircraft.

The truck was housed in a garage below the control tower. It held 400 gallons of water. With a turn of a knob, it could also spray foam when water alone would not put out the fire. The water cannon was located on top of the truck. With its 750 pounds of pressure, it could send spray shooting hundreds of feet through the air. It also had a 100-foot hand-held two-inch hose that served as a backup. But, the real responsibility, in the event of an emergency, was left in the hands of the airport's maintenance people.

Several months after we opened, I had two separate incidents happen while instructing the same student, Al Pagan.

Al was a quick learner and could handle the C-150 quite well. On this day we were above Boonton Reservoir, an area we often used as an area for practicing stalls, steep turns, and other required maneuvers. In the middle of the reservoir was a near perfectly round island which we used to practice turns about a point, helping to sharpen the student's coordination skills.

Normally, we would do our training no higher than 3000 feet. But that day we were at fifteen hundred feet doing steep 720s (going around in a circle twice while in a 45-degree steep bank) when off our left wing we spotted an airplane spinning downward near us. At first, I thought he was out of control. Then I realized he did it on purpose. I moved our practice area a mile or so from the reservoir. No sooner did we start our maneuvers again, then here comes this guy spinning downward. Only this time he's closer.

Now, I'm peeved, but play it safe and moved to another area. No sooner than we resumed our maneuvers we find this guy right behind our tail. Everywhere we turned, he followed. Al was getting more up-tight and I was not sure what this guy had in mind. I did a sharp climbing 180-degree turn, rolled level, and then another 180-degree turn and came up over the top of him. Once above him, I jotted down his aircraft registration number, located on his top wing, and followed him back to Towaco Airport which is several miles from Caldwell-Wright Airport. I then flew back to Wings.

I immediately called the FAA and reported the incident to Dick Klaus. He told me to file a complaint, which I did, and included that it was witnessed by my student. A week later, while sitting in flight operations, I received a telephone call from the pilot I filed the complaint against. He informed me that the FAA imposed a violation on him and he was being grounded for six months. He went on to say that he was just fooling around and I shouldn't have turned him in. The more he talked, the madder he got. He finally ended the conversation with, "I'm coming over to punch you in the mouth." I told him I'd be waiting. He never came over and I never did meet him.

Six months later I read in the newspaper about a fatal plane crash at Towaco Airport, right after the pilot took off. It seems the pilot hadn't flown his airplane in six months. The probable cause of the crash was water in the fuel tank. The guy who died in the accident was the same pilot who was going to punch me in the nose.

Many of the "water in fuel tank" accidents could have been avoided by following the procedure all pilots should do before they fly. First, do the proper walk-around inspection before each flight. This includes draining a small amount of fuel from the fuel tank sump drains located under each wing. It is simple: press upward on the drain by using a glass or clear plastic bottle designed for that purpose. As the fuel drains into the bottle, you will immediately know if there is any water in the tank.

Several weeks after that episode, there was another incident with Al Pagan. This time it was right after practicing stalls and slow flight over the reservoir. We were returning to the airport and entered the downwind portion of the traffic pattern for runway 31. That means you are parallel to the runway on which you are going to land. We had no operating control tower, so we were on our own. We noticed an aircraft had aborted its landing and started its go-around. Instead of falling in behind us, as he was supposed to do, getting back in line, he cut directly in front of us, close enough that I thought we might collide.

I banked to the right and pulled out of the traffic pattern, turned, and got back in line. In the meantime, the airplane that almost hit us aborted his landing again, and cut in front of us. I thought again we would collide. This time, instead of pulling out of line, I followed him down and landed behind him. He proceeded to the end of the runway and taxied down another runway. That would eventually lead him back to the runway from which he took off. And me!

Instead of following him, I taxied onto another runway (remember, we had three runways), the one he would have to use to get back to the active runway. When he saw I was blocking his path he finally stopped. When he did, I killed the engine on our aircraft and both Al and I jumped out and rushed to his plane. I yanked open the door of the four-place Cessna-172 and was about to let him know how close we came to having a mid-air collision. Several weeks before this incident, Sandy made me the Assistant Chief Pilot. One of my responsibilities was to inform pilots who I thought might need reminding, of our airport policies. That was what I had in mind with this character.

To my surprise, the pilot was Johnny Carson of late-night television fame. I noticed several men come running toward us. They turned out to be his television crew and were taping his first solo. This was his first solo.

At the time, I didn't know who was more scared. Al and me, when it seemed we were about to collide, or Johnny Carson, when I yanked his door open. My only comment on the incident was to tell him he needed to be more observant and not get that target fixation on landing. This occasionally happens when a pilot is so intent on doing one thing and doesn't realize what's happening around him. I let him know he had to be more aware of other aircraft in the traffic pattern and follow the airport's procedures and not cut in front of another aircraft.

For some reason, I don't know why, I reached into Johnny's seatback pocket, pulled out two sick sacks, and asked him to autograph them for us. To my surprise, he did.

I believe Al and I are probably the only two people in the world who have Johnny Carson's autograph on a sick sack. I still have mine. That night, during his television show, he showed the videotape of his first solo landing and taxiing back for another take-off. When our airplane started to come into view, the tape ended. However, I do believe somewhere in NBC's Archives, the entire tape would reveal how close we had come to crashing into one of entertainment's legendary stars.

The amusing thing before all this was I had seen Carson's camera crew standing on the grass near the runway but thought they were filming Curtiss-Wright's experimental aircraft, the X-19, which was parked on a nearby ramp.

The X-19 was a VOTOL, which stands for a Vertical Take-Off and Land-type aircraft that had high-mounted tandem wings. Each wing held two 13-foot tilting propellers that could rotate 90 degrees. The idea behind the four tilt-propeller driven X-19 was its ability to take off and land like a helicopter. As it took off and gained height, its propellers would rotate into a fixed position and fly like a fixed-wing aircraft. Its first flight was in November 1963. In August 1964, it crashed and was destroyed. Fortunately, there was no loss of life.

38

EXPLOSION

As a commercial pilot, when you are not flight instructing, you do get to do some unusual flying such as dumping human remains and ashes out of an airplane. Up to this time, I had never done that. This gentleman chartered Wings to disperse his father's remains over the Delaware Water Gap. I got the job.

I elected to use our four-seat C-172 thinking it would be more comfortable for him in that aircraft instead of the cramped two-seat C-150. We took off and headed west for the Gap with him sitting in the front right seat, next to me. As we flew toward the Delaware River, not much was said, but I could see him staring out the window as though lost in thought. As we approached the Gap, he pointed out the area where he wanted the ashes to be scattered, over the middle of the Gap.

I banked around and dropped down to 100 feet above the river. By that time, he opened the right front side window and held the urn halfway out, proceeding to dump his father's ashes. The good news was the ashes were going out over the Gap right where he wanted. The bad news? The propeller blast, combined with the aircraft's speed, created somewhat of a vacuum effect. A portion of his father's ashes was being sucked back into the C-172's back seat. Although most of the ashes were successfully scattered, it was sad watching him vacuum up what was left of his father's remnants when we returned to the airport.

May 7, 1963. A date that was literally burned into me. The sky was clear, the Northwest winds strong, with gusts of up to 25 miles per hour. A cold front had moved in that morning. Its swirling breezes felt cool and comfortable, a welcome relief from the day before. Because of the high winds, we had to cancel the students we had scheduled for that day. Nor were there any charter flights booked. Those types of days were reserved for catching up on ROTC and our other student's paperwork.

I had just grabbed a cup of coffee from our restaurant and walked outside the hangar when a tractor-trailer fuel tanker arrived a day earlier than normal. The tanker was carrying a full load of 5000 gallons of volatile 80/87 aviation fuel, of which, 1000 gallons were to be transferred to our near-empty 1000-gallon fuel truck. Our chief mechanic, Bill Hasselbeck, who usually handled the transfer, happened to have the day off.

Since Bill nor Sandy were available, and I was now the assistant chief pilot, the driver asked if I would help with the transfer. I looked at the driver and had this gut feeling. I hope he knows what he's doing, I thought. I replied that I never handled anything to do with transferring fuel. His response was, "Don't worry, I will be in charge and will tell you what to do."

One thing I did know from observing other fuel transfers in the past was that normally when a truck-to-truck transfer of fuel was in process, it was done by coupling at least a 20-foot-long, four-inch-wide hose from one truck to another. One end of the hose is attached to the bottom of the transferring truck and the other end is attached to the bottom of the receiving vehicle. The fuel is then pressure-fed into the receiving truck. One problem: he told me he did not have the proper attachments, but could still do the transfer by simply attaching the one hose he did bring with him to his truck and then sticking the other end down through the top of my truck's access hatch.

Reluctantly, I agreed but joked, "We better park our trucks away from the hangar, and from the aircraft that is parked nearby on the ramp. Just in case it blows up." Ha, ha.

We moved the trucks to the middle of the ramp and parked them side-by-side. He then detached the cab of his truck from the trailer. I thought that was strange. I had never seen other transfer drivers do that. But I climbed up on the top of my truck and opened the access hatch anyway. Once he attached the hose to the bottom of his truck, he handed me the other end.

That's when I noticed there was no shut-off nozzle, like the ones you see at gas stations. I asked him, "how do I shut off the fuel?" His answer: "Not a problem." He would control the flow of fuel by using a throttle in the cab of his truck. "When your truck is nearly full, let me know and I'll stop."

By that time, the Northwest wind and gusts were much stronger. I was still hesitant but stuck the end of the hose down inside my truck. I found I could only manage to get about four inches of it inside. Then I heard his truck engine start and then rev up as he played with the throttle.

At first, there was only a trickle of fuel coming from the hose into my truck. I told him that and he said he would increase the power. I heard his truck engine roar, followed by a blast of hot exhaust striking the left side of my body. I turned my head away from peering down inside the belly of my truck and spotted his truck's exhaust pipe. It ran up the right side of his cab, curved end pointing straight toward the open hatch.

I shouted, "turn off the truck!"

It was too late. Suddenly, everything became surreal.

From deep inside the belly of my truck came an enormous whooshing sound as though ten thousand cans of vacuumed-packed coffee burst open as the air inside was sucked out. That was followed by a great ball of fire ignited by the gas fumes inside the truck.

For a split second, I thought about slamming the hatch closed to smother the flames, but something warned me not to do that.

The limp four-inch-wide hose I was holding got rigid and popped out of the socket from the sudden pressure of the racing engine. What had been a trickle of gasoline became a roaring flame-thrower as hundreds of gallons of burning fuel were being pumped out.

The truck's engine was still at full power. I yelled at the people standing near my truck to get away as I held the hose as tight as I could, trying to prevent it from spraying them with fuel. They ran for their lives, but the pressure from the hose was enormous and I couldn't keep it from jerking side to side. Flaming fuel was spreading over the ramp. Aircraft engines were roaring to life. Their pilots had them at full throttle to get away from this erupting volcano. The large hangar doors were being slammed shut, preventing the burning river of fuel from entering.

The swirling winds that had been cool and comforting were now spraying deadly flames over me. Black oily smoke surrounded me. I held my breath, hoping I didn't inhale it, but I did. My clothes caught fire, as did my arms, pants, face, and my hair. I could smell that sickening acrid smell of flesh burning. My flesh! At any second, I expected the gas truck to explode. My only thought was, "This is one hell-of-a-way to die!"

Once I saw the people were cleared from the site, I let go of the hose and watched helplessly as the pressure made it snake back and forth, spewing more fuel and flame over the ramp. I began to whip the flames off my clothes, bare arms, and face. As though I was being guided by some other force, I leaped the six feet that separated the top of my truck to the top of the 5000-gallon truck that was upwind of the fire and flat-footed away from the inferno. Once I was clear, I dove off onto the pavement, jamming both hands, and rolled around on the asphalt smothering what flaming fuel was still on me.

As I lay on the ground, I peered underneath both trucks. All I could see were the legs of people running. They looked as though they were hanging from the bottom of the truck's chassis as if a puppeteer was controlling them. It was comical. No bodies, just legs. They were churning as fast as they could, and seemingly not going anywhere. I burst out laughing.

I picked myself up and looked back at the hellfire raging behind me. My truck was ablaze. The cab on the other driver's truck was on fire. The tanker had not yet caught fire. Fortunately, it was on the up-wind side and a distance away from where the fuel was still spewing out of the hose. The flame thrower was still lit. No one was around. I was alone.

Then I remembered, "Get to the crash truck!"

Still, in pain, I raced for the garage. Once inside I attempted to open the main garage door. It wouldn't budge. I decided to give it one more try. I told myself, "If I can't open it, I'll crash through the door with the fire truck."

The door finally opened. I drove the truck out and pulled up twenty feet from the burning fuel tanker. Jumping down from the cab, I ran to the side of the truck and opened the valves that would allow me to fight the fires with foam. I climbed to the top of the vehicle and began foaming down the blaze. Out of the corner of my eye, I caught a glimpse of the truck driver. He was running around in circles. I yelled to him and jumped off the fire truck, grabbed him by the arm, and dragged him back to its side. I gripped the 100-foot, two-inch hose and began unreeling it. I handed the end to him, telling him to aim it at the cab of his truck to try to put out the flames. That way he could reach in and shut the engine off to stop the fuel.

I climbed back into my truck. I looked to my left and saw a fountain of foam shooting straight up in the air. The driver had fainted and fell backward. As he lay there, the hose, still locked in his grip, was pointing skyward. Two people came from nowhere and dragged him out of the way.

To my surprise, the foam I was spraying was putting down the flames. I thought it looked like I had it under control. The foam ran out. The flames were back. The fuel truck was still pumping like a flame thrower.

I decided to try to get into the cab and kill the engine. Suddenly, I heard explosions. Each time it happened, I thought the trucks were exploding, and threw myself to the ground and covered my head.

Then I realized it was the truck's tires exploding from the flames. The cab was now fully engulfed in fire. No way can I kill the engine, I thought. Are those sirens I hear?

The sirens got louder. The local fire department showed up and took over.

I sat down on the ramp, ready to cry. I was hustled into an EMS truck and raced to the hospital. I ended up with first, second, and third-degree burns, smoke inhalation, and two sprained wrists. The doctors were amazed that I was not permanently scarred. I was more amazed. And thankful.

Was it continually wiping away the flames from my clothes, my arms, and my face that prevented my being scarred for life? Or, was it my guardian angels or the grace from a higher power that kept me from being roasted alive and becoming another accident statistic?

When I was released from the hospital, that same evening, one of the instructors came there to drive me back to the airport and then home.

Barbara was not made aware of what happened until later that night. In the car with us was the fuel truck driver. He too was taken to the hospital in another ambulance and was released without any injuries.

As one of our instructors was talking about what they witnessed, the other driver was in the back seat smoking a cigarette. He leaned forward to listen and accidentally burned the back of my neck with his cigarette. If I could have made a fist, I probably would have punched him in the jaw. But because both wrists were severely strained, I couldn't do anything.

This driver said they were watching me kneeling on top of the truck when it erupted in a ball of fire, and I disappeared into the flames. "We all thought you burned to death," he said.

The next question everyone wanted to be answered was what prevented the trucks from blowing up. After the investigation was concluded weeks later, the investigating team said, had I closed the hatch on top of my truck, the fire inside would have probably caused an explosion of the fuel truck. If that happened, shrapnel most likely would have penetrated the other fuel tanker. Then, it too would have probably exploded.

I was later sued by the owner of the tanker, E. Brooke Matlock, and by the driver-owner of the truck. We did go to a jury, and the jury found E. Brooke Matlock and its driver guilty of negligence and ordered them to pay for all damages. That included our truck, airport property, the ramp, and other damages. I was later told that the owner of the cab had no insurance on his $20,000 cab. My thought at the time was, too bad. I received a nominal amount, less than $1,000.00 for the burns I got, from the insurance company. My loss of work and medical bills were covered under the workman's compensation. Pain and suffering, at that time, weren't a consideration. After that incident, any time a load of fuel came in, someone else handled it. I thanked my guardian angel again.

39

THE DUMP

During the summer of 1963, our student and charter flying picked up by increasing our advertising. Occasionally, Chet and Sandy would revise our flight brochure, which listed our student and charter rates. On our new brochure, they wanted a photograph of our twin-engine Piper Apache on its cover with me as its pilot and a passenger shown boarding.

For the photo shoot, I stood on the walkway of the right wing with a suitcase in hand and appeared to be stepping into the cockpit. My passenger stood next to the wing. We both smiled and looked at the camera. The shot was taken. Afterward, the supposed passenger invited me for a cup of coffee in our restaurant. We sat down and he lay open a large briefcase that he had with him. While I sipped my coffee, he removed a sheet of blank paper and started drawing. With quick flashes of his wrist and hand, he finished, signed the drawing, and gave it to me.

It was a sketch of a puppet I had seen many times while watching television. The artist was Milt Neil. The puppet: Howdy Doody.

Milt Neil owned and kept his airplane at the airport, so he was no stranger to us flight instructors. His fame derived from being a character animator for Disney Studios for many years. Some of the animated movies he worked on were Dumbo, Fantasia, Snow White, and The Seven Dwarfs, and that character that, at times, had trouble holding his temper, Donald Duck. Milt also carried the title, "The Official Artist of the Howdy Doody Show." The show was hosted by Buffalo Bob Smith. I felt very flattered to have a photograph taken with Neal and of the drawing.

As the summer of "63" wore on, there were more students and more flying. One day a guy came into the office who wanted to continue to take flying lessons. It seems he was taking flying lessons from Hanover Airport which was several miles away. As we talked, he started to tell me his instructor was showing him what to do in case of an engine failure before he would allow him to solo. In other words, practice forced landings. This guy didn't think it was necessary. I asked him who his instructor was. He said, Glenn Frister. I said he's my brother and he's right, and if you decide to fly here at Wings, you'll be shown how to do forced landings before you solo. He walked out the door.

Several months later, he came back and had trouble walking because of the crutches under both arms. Then he proceeded to tell me what happened. It seems he did get his private pilot's license at another airport, but it wasn't at Hanover. After that, he decided to buy an airplane, a French airplane. The representative pilot, who was to demonstrate the aircraft, took off on a very windy day from Hanover Airport. The guy was in the front right seat with two other passengers in the back seat. Right after the lift-off, the engine quit. The plane crashed, its nose buried in the ground. The pilot doing the demonstration was killed on impact, and the two people in the back seat had non-life-threatening injuries. The guy who didn't think practicing forced landings was necessary had his legs crushed and most likely would be unable to walk for the rest of his life.

While he was telling me all this, I could tell that he had no sympathy for the dead pilot because of the injuries he incurred. The reason he stopped by to see me was to let me know that had the demonstrating pilot known how to handle a forced landing, he wouldn't be walking on crutches. I guess some people have to learn the hard way.

Meteorologically speaking, summer brings on hot and muggy days. With that comes intense thunderstorms, heavy rains, bolts of lightning, and severe winds. And as often happens in hot and muggy weather come temperature inversions. Inversions happen when the temperature increases with height instead of decreasing. Thereby, pollutants get trapped below that line where the inversion is, and in turn, we get those hazy lazy days of summer.

Pilot-wise, if you have an inversion, the pollutants in the air reduce your forward visibility drastically. That means if you're flying into the sun, your visibility may be less than a half mile, even though your weatherman may have predicted you would have five miles of visibility flying. You'll still be able to see straight down, or up, and to your left and right, but with a varied reduction in distance.

On one of my few days off, I received a telephone call at home from Wings. It involved one of my students who was supposed to be on what we called a "round-robin" solo cross-country flight. That meant flying from one airport to another, then another, and then returning to Caldwell Airport.

"He's had an accident. But, he's okay. The airplane, on the other hand, is in the Secaucus Dump," Sandy said.

"What!"

I jumped into my car and hightailed it to the airport. When I arrived, Sandy and Bill were waiting for me. We jumped into Bill's truck, already packed with the necessary tools and parts to fix the damage. As we raced for the dump, Sandy filled me in on what happened. I was stunned.

The day before my student's cross-country flight, I left word with one of our instructors working that day, not to let him go unless he had clear skies and more than five miles of visibility.

In all fairness to the instructor, he did check the weather with my student long before he was to start the cross-country. At the time, the skies were clear, and visibility was more than five miles. The instructor thought it would be okay for him to go because my student had flown solo cross-countries before. But the weather has a bad habit of changing when you least expect it.

According to Sandy, Ralph, my student, told him he was supposed to take off around 8 that morning but was delayed for almost an hour and took off around 9 a.m. Once airborne, he climbed and crossed over Caldwell Airport on the proper heading for his first intended landing, Mercer County Airport in Trenton, NJ. The heading would be approximately 135 degrees. Not quite, but almost directly into the rising sun.

Ralph said that once he was beyond Caldwell Airport, he became disoriented because of the sun's glare and a haze level thicker than forecast. All of which brought his forward visibility to less than a mile and he found himself between Teterboro and Newark airport. Then he saw the heavy airline traffic flying near him as planes were making their approach to land. He panicked, thinking they might collide with him.

Ralph saw a dirt road below and landed on it. Luckily, he didn't bust up the airplane, or himself. The only damage was to one of the brakes, and that was because he was pressing on them when he landed, hoping to get the airplane stopped before it nosed into the garbage piles.

Ralph left the airplane in the dump, walked out, crossed the heavily trafficked Route 3 highway, went to Howard Johnson's, and called Wings. Then he went to a car rental agency and drove home.

After Bill repaired the brake, the next question was how do we get this airplane out of the dump without disassembling it, or letting the FAA know about it? The latter would have led to a lot of questions about letting a student pilot fly under such visibility circumstances, training, and all the rest that goes with it when they conduct their investigations.

I told Sandy since it was my student who put the plane there, I would be the one who would fly it out and back to Caldwell. The only problem the dirt road my student landed on was narrow, and winding, and its length was probably no more than 500 to 600 hundred feet. Oh, yes. The road led back to the main highway and traffic.

This was not going to be easy.

40

THE WAITING GAME

O ur plan was to have Sandy and Bill stop the garbage trucks and other cars from entering the dump. We asked those who were already there to pull off the dirt road far enough so my plane's wings wouldn't strike them as I took off. Everyone cooperated but was scratching their heads, wondering what an airplane was doing in their dump.

Once the area was clear, we turned the C-150 around and faced it in the direction in which I was going to take off. Then we pushed it back as far as we could, the tail and wings almost touching the mounds of trash. I climbed into the cockpit and started the engine, keeping both feet firmly on the brakes, and making sure that if I had to suddenly stop, the brakes were going to work. Almost immediately, there was a dust storm, dirt and cinders swirling around the airplane from the propeller blast.

I dropped my flaps to do this short-field take-off. I did my usual pre-takeoff check, checked the Mag's, then pushed the throttle in. With the engine at full power, just like a plane on an aircraft carrier ready for launch, I released the brakes and started down the dirt road.

With the engine at full power, the clouds of dirt and dust from the prop wash became thicker and obstructed my forward view. I looked out the side window and kicked the left and right rudders to stay on the winding road. In what seemed like an eternity, I gained enough speed and lifted off, glancing down as I did. The truck drivers were waving and jumping up and down as I crossed over them. For a moment I felt like Charles Lindbergh on his arrival in Paris after he crossed the Atlantic Ocean alone.

Once airborne, my forward visibility was limited because of the haze but I breathed a sigh of relief that all was well. That is until I saw the high-voltage powerlines directly in front of me. That was something we could not see from our position at the dump.

Here I was at low altitude, hanging on the prop, flying just a few knots above stall speed. I can't make a bank for fear of stalling out. I was in big trouble, but it's amazing how quickly your mind reacts. "If I elect to go under the wires, will the tail of the C-150 catch one of them? If I go over, will the landing gear catch one of them?"

I pushed the nose down, skimmed over the ground to gain more airspeed, then, just before hitting the wires, pulled back on the control column. I skimmed over the top of the wires and pushed the nose down again, my landing gear nearly touching the weeds of the Meadowland Swamp. I then got my speed back, started climbing, and flew back to Caldwell Airport.

If Sandy or Bill ever saw how close I came to those wires, they never let on. Sandy did tell me he thought it was a terrific piece of flying. That made me feel great. I never told them how close I came to hitting those wires.

Wings charged my student for the flying time and damage to the airplane. The FAA never became involved, nor was there any report of the airplane ever landing in the dump. Ralph quit flying after that incident.

As our flight school expanded, Chet hired a young mechanic, Vic Var-cardipone to help take the workload off Bill. Vic, as did Richie Green, Vic Quinto, and myself, wanted to fly for an airline. He had a private pilot's certificate and a multi-engine rating and was working to obtain his commercial pilot's certificate. When he received that, the next step would be to get his flight instructor's certificate to help build his required flight time. On occasion, we'd sit down and have a cup of coffee together and discuss flying.

Over time, Vic Quinto had been building his flight hours. One day, Vic and I were discussing some of our students and the problems that might arise. As we were talking, one of the aircraft owners, based at Caldwell, walked by. Once he was out of earshot, Vic said. "There's an accident waiting to happen."

I asked him what he meant. He told me he had seen things that this guy did, and thought that at times, he wasn't aware of what was going on around him, especially in the air traffic pattern.

My reply was that it could be the guy, but maybe it's because we did not have an operating control tower, and some pilots get a little too complacent.

I don't believe ten days passed when the person we had been discussing (who owned a C-172, which is a high-wing aircraft) landed on top of a Mooney Mark 21 (a low-wing aircraft) just as they were both touching down on the same runway. The propeller of the C-172 chopped its way up the Mark 21's fuselage and stopped right at the back of the pilot's headrest. They both lost control of their airplanes and swerved off the runway into the grass. Incredibly, neither was injured.

But you have to wonder why the pilot of the "high-wing" did not see the guy in the "low-wing" plane. When asked, he answered, "He must have been in my blind spot."

Sometime during the summer, Vic Qunito received good news about a flying position. It seems some musician-guitarist-singer needed an additional pilot to fly him and his group around the country. Wherever the city was, Vic would fly him there. Part of his job also required him to set up the speakers, microphones, and whatever else was needed for the group to perform. I was happy for him and wished him a lot of luck.

Vic flew for this group for quite a while, and it just so happened that I was at the airport when he walked into the hangar with a guitar in hand. He said it belonged to the guitarist and he gave it to him. As I remember, as he showed it to me, he pointed out that it was an electric guitar the musician had used at one of his concerts. The guitar was beautiful with a sunburst design on its front. I told him it was nice, but never asked him if he knew how to play the guitar.

And oh. The musician's name. Bob Dylan.

Today that electric guitar is worth hundreds of thousands of dollars.

Unfortunately, Vic passed away long before knowing what its full value would be in today's market.

Meanwhile, for me, flight training still went on. Many of my students had finished their flight training, passed the written exams, took their flight tests with the FAA, and were now private pilots. But the door was still revolving. New students, same mistakes.

One of my students, Reese, was a gentle giant. He had hands the size of a catcher's mitt. I had given him many hours of instruction and he was now ready for his solo. The one problem he always seemed to have would be on the downwind leg of the landing, at that point, where you would normally pull out the black knob (carburetor heat) which would direct hot engine heat around the carburetor. The reason you do that is to help prevent carburetor icing due to moisture and cold weather. If you don't, there is always a possibility of carburetor icing and the engine may quit.

Right next to the black knob is a red knob (mixture control) for controlling the right amount of fuel-to-air ratio mixture to the carburetor. In simpler terms: When you get to your cruising altitude you pull out the mixture control until you see a slight drop in RPMs, then stop. This means you will have less gas consumption and more range. It's also another way to kill the engine, other than turning off the magnetos.

It seemed each time we were on the downwind leg, Reese would reach over and pull out the red knob. After a few seconds, the engine would start sputtering. In goes the mixture control, the engine roars back to life, and out comes the black knob. We're safe.

Finally, the day for Reese to solo had arrived. We did a couple of take-offs and landings. All went well. I get out of the airplane and away he goes. Meanwhile, Vic Quinto comes over and stands in the grass next to me. Nothing is said as we watch my student turn onto the downwind leg. Right where you would normally put the heat on, the engine starts sputtering and sounds as if it is about to quit. Then it roars back to life.

Vic looks at me and says, "Whom are you soloing? Reese?"

"Yup," I reply.

Reese makes a perfect landing. I wave for him to do a couple of more take-offs and landings to a full stop.

All are perfect. The engine on the downwind leg doesn't miss a beat. My heart missed a few beats instead.

As we rolled into Autumn of 63, the weather began to change. The warm days of summer were being replaced with dreary periods of rainy and cold weather and student cancellations. The sun now set at 5 p.m. instead of 9 p.m. and you lose four more hours of precious flying time.

New applications go out. Rejections come back. More gloom is on the horizon. Christmas is less than six weeks away and another birthday, number twenty-seven.

It was one of those nasty days of cold and rain, low visibility, and fog that forced me to cancel what students I had. It meant another dent would show up in my paycheck for that week.

I had just finished having a conversation with Bill and Vic, our mechanics, about one of our C-150s and was walking through the hangar when Sandy and another gentleman entered.

Sandy introduced him to me. His name was Pete Coxhead, a first officer who flew for Eastern Air Lines and just happened to stop by. I'm thrilled. Sandy then gets called away.

I tell Pete that I always wanted to fly for Eastern ever since I was a kid. We talked for almost an hour about flying, my experience, and my number of flying hours. He took my name and told me he would send Eastern a recommendation for me. I gave him my thanks but did not believe he would do that.

Several weeks later, I received, much to my surprise, a letter from Eastern Air Lines to come to Miami for an interview on the recommendation of Pete Coxhead. Eastern sent me an airline pass and I flew down to Miami for the interview.

It was more than just an interview. It encompassed a series of written tests, mostly on my knowledge of navigation, and weather, along with other factors, and a psychological test. After the testing, came the interview with Captain O. B. Bevins who had the final say on my being hired.

It started with him saying, "Let's see your pilot's logbooks." I had brought the log with me and we went through the entire book. This was followed by more questions with me providing more answers. Captain Bevins nodded as if in agreement with my responses.

The interview finally came to an end. As I stood up to leave we shook hands and he said, "Eastern Air Lines thinks very highly of First Officer Pete Coxhead." I was not sure what he meant, but said a silent prayer to myself, and left.

I flew back home. The waiting game began.

Weeks passed. Nothing.

December 5th, birthday number 27, comes and goes. As do Christmas and New Year's. January 1964 enters cold and snowy. I was in my last year of eligibility for any airline, age-wise.

Not hearing from Eastern, flight instructing goes on.

January 3rd. I'm to instruct one of my students, Bob Bottoni, on a cross-country flight to an airport that he and I had never been to. A flight that came close to being my last.

41

LAST SHOT

Snuggled in the hills just west-northwest of the city of Strasburg, Pennsylvania, is Hamlin Airport, some fifteen miles away. Hamlin is one of those old country styles: old-fashioned, one runway grass strip airports. It was like many of the hundreds of small out-of-the-mainstream airports at that time.

It had snowed a couple of days before, but now, once the front passed, the skies were clear, the wind cold and blustery and the visibility unlimited. It was a beautiful day to fly. That is if you didn't mind being bounced around in turbulence.

Normally, I wouldn't have flown on a day like this, but I had an advanced student and I thought it would give him a lot of confidence in his flying ability for a couple of reasons. One, he would be able to handle take-off and landings in blustery conditions; and two, he would be able to locate a country airport out in the middle of nowhere that was covered with snow. Whether we would land or not depended on the condition of the runway.

Bottoni had no trouble finding Hamlin. As we flew over it, he called Hamlin's Unicom. As we crossed over it, we could see that the narrow runway was plowed with high snowbanks bordering each side. The Unicom operator informed us of wind direction and velocity.

The wind was coming from the northwest directly across the runway with gusts of up to 15 miles per hour. That is about the maximum for a crosswind take-off and landing for the C-150.

I decided that Bottoni was capable of a safe landing. He made the approach as he was supposed to do in a crosswind landing: wing down on the up-wind side with the use of rudder and aileron, so the wind won't push the aircraft sideways to end up in a snowbank. He made a nice approach and landed. We taxied to the small parking area next to the flight shack and he killed the engine.

Once we were inside, I found the man who had talked to us on the Unicom. It turned out he was Mr. Hamlin, the owner of the airport. We grabbed a cup of coffee and enjoyed our conversation of about twenty minutes, which was just long enough to warm up. We then returned to our airplane. In the meantime, another pilot radioed in and said he was going to land at the airport.

Hamlin started to walk out to our airplane with us just as the other airplane landed. He told us to go ahead and crank up our engine while he contacts the landing aircraft by Unicom and tells him to stay at the plowed-out turn-around area at the end of the runway, so we can leave.

I agreed with this. The problem: most grass-strip runways don't have taxiways, so you have to taxi back on the active runway you landed on. In addition, most grass strip runways are not always level. Unfortunately, this runway, instead of being flat, had an arc to it so severe that we were unable to see the other end from where we were going to start our take-off run.

By this time, the wind had increased, and the gusts were higher and more than I thought my student could handle. I told him that I would do the take-off. He happily concurred.

I went through the normal engine check of the mags, left, right, and both. I checked the tachometers, and ran through the usual flexing of the controls of the rudder, ailerons, and elevator, making sure nothing had frozen up from all that blowing snow that was coming off the snowbanks. All well, I pushed the throttle to full and started down the runway.

Because of the heavy crosswinds coming from our right, I had to hold a lot of right rudder and right aileron to keep from drifting into the snowbanks on our left. Just as we lift off, over the hill, and coming straight at us, is the airplane that was supposed to stay where he was.

I'm barely above flying speed with nowhere to go. If I chop power and land, we'll collide head-on. I don't have enough height to fly over the top of him. Another split-second decision.

Wait, wait, time it.

Bottoni covers his face waiting for the impact.

At the last second, I do a steep bank to the right to get my left wing up. As I do, his left wing goes under my left wing, narrowly missing my left wing strut. My right wheel catches the top of the plowed snowbank. The right wing makes contact with the snow-covered ground. The nose of the aircraft pitches downward at what seems to be a nearly 45-degree angle. The propeller slices through the snow like the action of a snow-blower and covers our windshield and fuselage. As we're about to flip over on our back, a stronger gust of wind strikes us. We hold that near-vertical position for what seems like an eternity, then get hammered by another burst which slams us back down on the main landing gear. As we sit on top of the snowbank, I kill the engine and dread the thought of the damage.

Bottoni and I exited the cockpit and take an assessment of the C-150. Nothing? No damaged wing. No damaged prop. Incredible! Relief starts to turn into anger.

The pilot of the other airplane had stopped, killed the engine on his Piper Tri-Pacer, and came running over. He said he was from Syracuse, New York, and apologized profusely as he shook Bottoni and my hands for what nearly became a deadly head-on collision. He said he thought we were waiting for him because we didn't take off right away and that was why he started taxing down the runway.

Hamlin comes charging up the runway. I take one look at him and could see he was beside himself at what could have been a disaster. He was very apologetic.

The anger faded. I made another "amen" to my guardian angels. We moved the C-150 off the snowbank and hopped back in our airplane. We went through our flight check as though nothing happened, take off, and head back to Caldwell Airport. The aircraft performed beautifully. No vibrations from anything being bent out of shape, just the usual turbulence.

When we returned to Wings, I told our mechanic what happened and asked him to check the airplane for any structural damage. There was none. I informed Sandy of the incident, and he told me since the FAA wasn't involved, not to worry about it.

I wasn't worried about this incident. It was over. What I was concerned with was my income. I felt I had enough flying hours in my flight logbook for any airline, but that did not seem to be happening. It was painfully obvious, even that being a full-time flight instructor was not paying enough, especially now that winter was in full swing. I had always had a backup plan if flying for an airline was not in the cards. I would look for a career that could provide a good income, a pension, paid vacations, medical coverage, and allow me to be home every night.

I knew I could probably get a job back at the Dover Post Office delivering mail during the week. Then I could instruct part-time on the weekends or my days off. As yet, I had not heard anything from Eastern.

Finally, I made my decision. I gave Sandy my two weeks' notice. I would fly with several more of my students during those two weeks. Then another instructor would take my place.

On January 12, 1964, I flew with Mr. Konefat in C-150 N6608T. He would be the last student I would instruct. After one hour of doing take-offs and landings, along with some radio instruction, my days as a flight instructor came to an end.

Ten days after I began working for the post office, I received a telegram from Eastern Air Lines. Was the answer from them a yes, or a no? I took a deep breath, opened and read the telegram:

YOU HAVE BEEN ACCEPTED FOR PILOT EMPLOYMENT WITH EAL COMMENCING JAN 27, 1964. YOUR PRE-EMPLOYMENT PHYSICAL HAS BEEN SET UP FOR JAN 24, 1964 AT 9:30 A.M. LETTER OF INSTRUCTIONS FOLLOWS. PLEASE CONFIRM EMPLOYMENT. R.P. RORDAM PILOT EMPLOYMENT EASTERN AIR LINES.

My lifelong dream was about to come true.

Stay Turned for Book 2

I enjoyed my adventurous life. Now I was close to my dream of becoming an airline pilot. Would I succeed in facing the challenges of an airline pilot, where others have failed? This is my true story of how I reached for my dreams and sometimes stumbled. Please stay with me as we travel the bumpy roads and try to soar higher in the sky. Thank you for hanging on for the next leg of the journey. Don't forget to buckle your seatbelt.

Thank you,
RAF (Not the Royal Air Force) Bob

About the Author

Captain Robert Allen Frister was born in Dover, New Jersey, in 1936. Upon graduating from high school, he spent three years in the Navy, he was with an antisubmarine-bomber patrol squadron and then, later on, with a lighter-than-air blimp squadron. Afterward, he attended Parks Air College in Illinois, graduating in 1958.

He was a flight instructor and charter pilot before joining Eastern Air Lines as a co-pilot. In 1970, he was the co-pilot who flew the flight that set a world speed record, flying from Houston to Newark, New Jersey, in a B-727, That record still stands.

Bob's two sons, Scott Frister, and Keith Frister are now captains with United Airlines (Scott) and Southwest Airlines (Keith). It is also interesting to note that there are a total of twelve (12) pilots in the Frister family. A family record.

Presently, he is living in The Villages, Florida with his wife Barbara (Barb).

Made in United States
Orlando, FL
07 January 2023